BURGUNDY

Other books by John Flower

Provence
Lombardy

BURGUNDY

John Flower

AURUM PRESS

First published 1994 by Aurum Press Limited,
25 Bedford Avenue, London WC1B 3AT
Copyright © 1994 by John Flower

All rights reserved. No part of this book may be
reproduced or utilized in any form or by any means,
electronic or mechanical, including photocopying,
recording or by any information storage and retrieval
system, without permission in writing from
Aurum Press Limited.

The right of John Flower to be identified as Author
of this work has been asserted by him
in accordance with the Copyright, Design
and Patents Act 1988.

A catalogue record for this book is available
from the British Library

ISBN 1 85410 280 X

2 4 6 8 10 9 7 5 3 1

1995   1997   1998   1996   1994

Design by Don Macpherson
Map by John Gilkes
Illustration by Don Macpherson
Typeset by Wyvern Typesetting Ltd, Bristol
Printed and bound in Great Britain by
Hartnolls Ltd., Bodmin

*À la petite
communauté marrésienne.*

Contents

General map of Burgundy   viii
Acknowledgements   x

Introduction   1

1   The Northern Approaches   10

2   Dijon   53

3   The Golden Trail   76

4   The Pull of the Midi   98

5   La France profonde   127

6   In and around the Morvan   149

Index   180

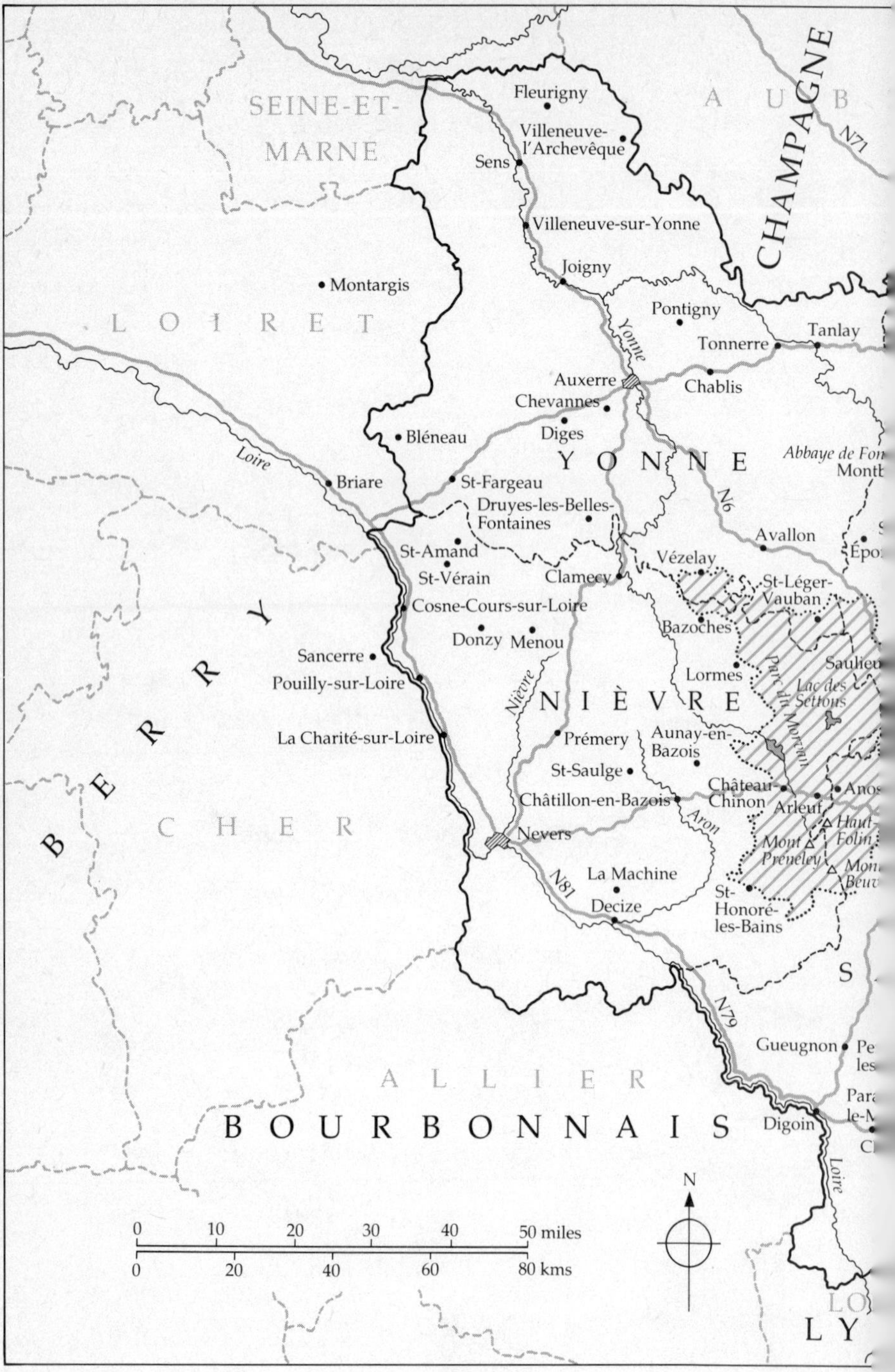

SEINE-ET-MARNE
AUBE
CHAMPAGNE
N71
Fleurigny
Villeneuve-l'Archevêque
Sens
Villeneuve-sur-Yonne
Joigny
Montargis
LOIRET
Pontigny
Tonnerre
Tanlay
Yonne
Auxerre
Chablis
Chevannes
Diges
Bléneau
YONNE
Abbaye de Fon
Montb
Loire
Briare
St-Fargeau
N6
Druyes-les-Belles-Fontaines
Avallon
Épo
St-Amand
Vézelay
St-Vérain
Clamecy
St-Léger-Vauban
Cosne-Cours-sur-Loire
Donzy
Menou
Bazoches
BERRY
Sancerre
Saulieu
Pouilly-sur-Loire
Lormes
Parc du Morvan
Lac des Settons
Nièvre
NIÈVRE
La Charité-sur-Loire
Prémery
Aunay-en-Bazois
St-Saulge
Château-Chinon
Anos
Châtillon-en-Bazois
Arleuf
Haut-Folin
Aron
CHER
Nevers
Mont Préneley
Mon Beuv
N81
La Machine
St-Honoré-les-Bains
Decize
S
N79
Gueugnon
Pe les
ALLIER
Para le-M
BOURBONNAIS
Digoin
Loire
N
0 10 20 30 40 50 miles
0 20 40 60 80 kms
LO
LY

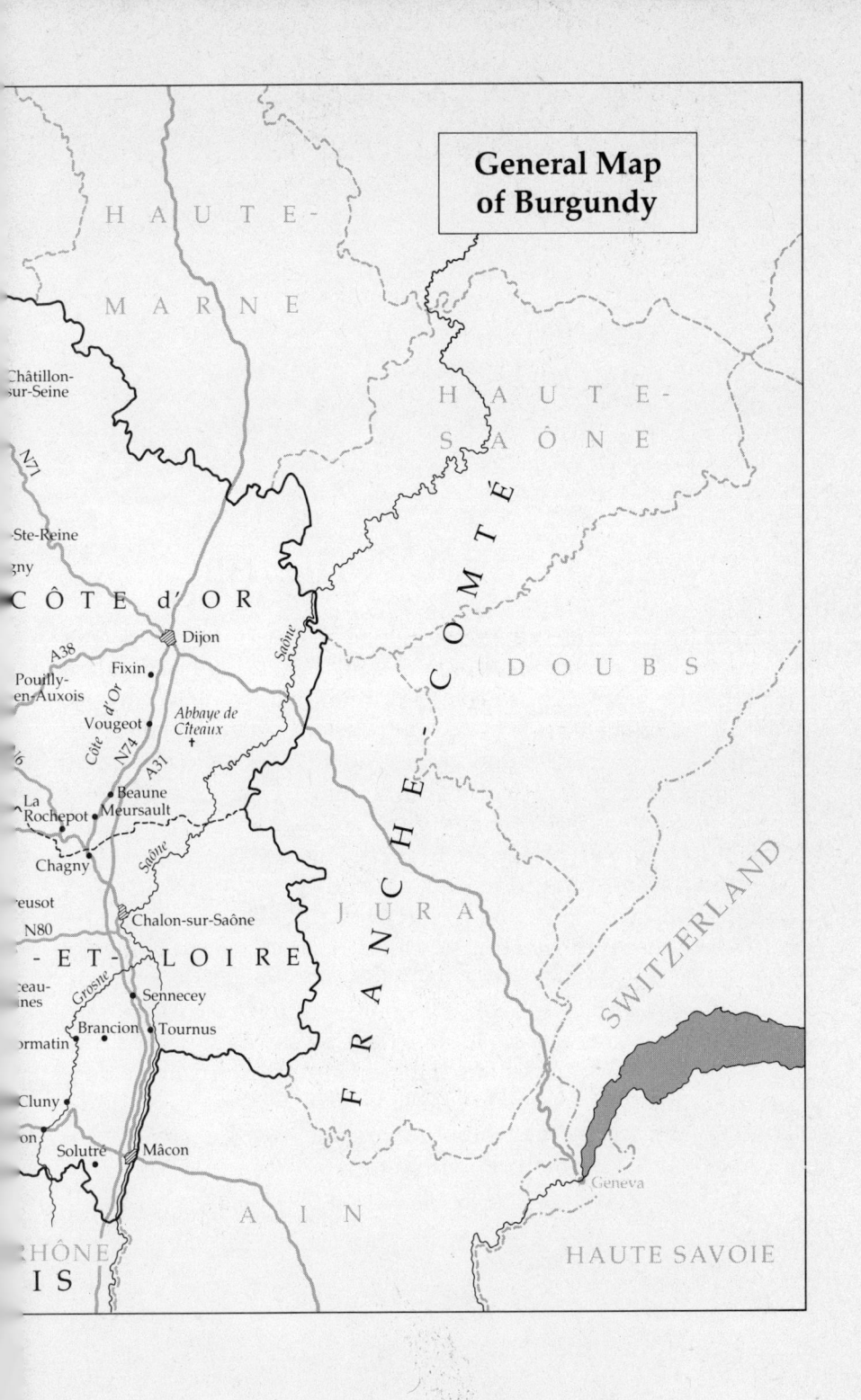

General Map of Burgundy

Acknowledgements

To thank by name all who have helped me (wittingly or not) in the preparation of this book is impossible. *Syndicats d'initiative* and *offices de tourisme* throughout Burgundy have plied me with material, introduced me to people whose local, specialized knowledge has been invaluable and managed to unlock several doors which appeared at first to be firmly shut. A number of hotel owners, *vignerons*, farmers, and even colleagues – all of whom, they will no doubt be pleased to hear, remain clad in anonymity – have, at different times, provided me with pieces of information I would have been fortunate to discover elsewhere. It would be most remiss of me, however, not to express my warmest thanks in particular to a small group of friends in deepest Burgundy whose interest and hospitality have been immense: Annie and David Bancroft and Raymond and Jannine Legall. I should like also to thank Sara Moore for her exemplary word-processing skills, and finally my family, who have followed the progress of this book, sometimes with amusement but with growing and – dare I say – irreversible commitment.

John Flower

Introduction

I am not sure I can remember when or where I first came across the name Burgundy. Probably, like most people, it was on the label on a bottle of wine which equally probably was drunk with little reflection or attention to taste. Certainly further acquaintance was through wine. I recall being told that Clos de Vougeot was 'a Burgundy' and I think I may have known by then that so were Beaune and Meursault. Later, trips to the south of France meant that I could conveniently pass through these mysterious places and so they became real. Furthermore, on the advice of friends in Paris I began to buy wine from recommended *vignerons* and so entered a world whose complexity continues to baffle me. One glum, taciturn *vigneron* in Vosne-Romanée produced a rich, dark wine which, when the bottle was opened, smelled (as it should) of the dung heap. Another, a delightful elderly gentleman in Chassagne-Montrachet, recognized my interest and eventually took me to the most private of the cellars beneath his house, where new wine would be left quietly to mature and be regularly sampled. It was in his main cellar that I met others of his generation and we talked about the Resistance in Burgundy as enthusiastically as we did about his wine. Sadly, he died a few years ago and his son, equally skilled but more of a modern business man, has developed the property – and the prices. And there were bigger producers, like the Baron Thénard in Givry whose holdings are considerable, whose wine is variable but some of which is very reliable. Even quite sizeable commercial *caves co-opératives* like the one in Gamay became part of the circuit, where the constant stream of local people armed with wicker-clad glass *bonbonnes* or plastic *cubitainers* testified, and still does, to the reliability of the wine (*supérieur* or *ordinaire*) taken from huge barrels like petrol.

Gradually my acquaintance with Burgundy developed and to these ports of call have in particular been added Fixin, Meursault, Auxey-Duresses and Poncey, where a combination of quality, price and a genuine welcome can mean that the journey from Dijon to, say, Chalon, has to be planned carefully in advance and cannot be completed in a hurry. (A word of advice, too. If you plan to visit a *vigneron* during the summer avoid arriving between midday and three o'clock: lunch and siesta time are sacred.) Such an introduction to Burgundy is by no means unique, of course. Thousands have made the same transition from bottle (and its contents) to place and have their favourite villages and growers. And those who are familiar with the sprawling vineyards of the Bordeaux region will be struck by the neatness and limited size of the Burgundian *clos*. They may also notice how much more quickly, in general, Burgundy becomes ready for drinking than the initially unyielding wine from the Cabernet Sauvignon grape in the south-west.

As a glance at any map denoting the wine areas of France will soon make clear, an acquaintance with this region south of Dijon by no means exhausts Burgundy's potential. To the north-west of it lies Chablis, perhaps the best known white wine name in the world; further west on the Loire is Pouilly; to the south are the villages around Mâcon, and beyond them Pouilly-Fuissé. There are also literally dozens of other tiny villages producing red, white, rosé and even sparkling wines, though often in insufficient quantity to be viable on any real commercial scale.

But a map will also show you that even if the major wine-producing areas of Burgundy were removed a great deal remains. This is one of France's most varied and complex regions, with a landscape made up of extensive forests (of which the Morvan is one of France's best), windswept plateaux, deep, near-impenetrable valleys, and vast areas of undulating arable and pasture land yellow with sunflowers or rape, white with cherry blossom, golden with corn, deep brown when freshly ploughed or dotted with the huge, statuesque creamy-white Charolais cattle for which the region has become renowned. Skies wiped clean by fierce winds, banks of storm clouds, sudden squalls, periods of intense dry heat or of sub-zero temperatures all contribute to this variety. Nor, for all that it has one of the lowest population densities in France, is Burgundy simply rural. Towns like Auxerre, Sens, Tournus, Nevers or Mâcon, for example, are rich in history, and dozens of villages retain their beautiful, compact Romanesque churches, some with their roofs covered by intricately patterned polychrome tiles, others by huge, flat stones. This is also a region of châteaux of all sizes, descriptions and ages, from massive fortified buildings, little altered since the twelfth century and with the scars of siege and battle almost still visible, to elegant seventeenth- and eighteenth-century residences, tributes to a more peaceful age, their delicate carving and plasterwork carefully preserved and their interiors often beautifully furnished. Some have remained in the hands of the same family for generations, others, damaged at the time of the Revolution, have been bought and sold, and in certain cases have only been rescued in the late twentieth century by a mixture of sensible investment (by state and *département*) and the enterprise of imaginative and wealthy individuals. At Fontenay, Cîteaux and Cluny are the sites of three of the world's great monasteries, and at Autun, Auxerre and Sens some of the finest cathedrals certainly in France and even in Europe. And then there is Dijon, in my view one of the most delightful and elegant of regional capitals in all of France.

When, in 1964, President De Gaulle reintroduced the notion of regions into France, Burgundy was, in a sense, reborn. In its modern form it embraces four *départements*, Yonne, Côte d'Or, Nièvre and Saône-et-Loire – a far cry from the years in the Middle Ages when its territories ranged from near the Swiss border to the Channel. But such a neat division, however convenient administratively, is even today only a guide and is certainly not considered by all those who consider themselves Burgundians to be in any way accurate. Along the northern approaches it is useful, as the characteristics of the Île de France and Champagne gradually, imperceptibly dissolve and become something different. To the west the Loire is a natural border, but the area north-west around Montargis has features we can find much nearer the interior of Burgundy. To the east the Saône is equally a natural border. Beyond it the region of Bresse is staunchly defended by its inhabitants and in the very south people living beyond a line roughly from Paray-le-Monial to just south of Mâcon will declare their allegiance to the Brionnais. Within Burgundy, too, there are smaller areas, each with its own particular geographical, natural and climatic characteristics. Some, like the Côte or the Mâconnais with their limestone escarpments, or the Morvan with its forest and almost constant rain outside the height of summer, are well known; others are less so. In the north the Senonais with its rich lands resembles the great fertile expanses of the Brie, but the transition between it and the clay and sandy soil of the Gâtinais is abrupt. Here and in the upper parts of the Puisaye immediately to the south you find some of the poorest land in Burgundy, despite a good deal of surface water in the form of small tributaries of the Loiret or of ponds (*mares*) or larger expanses sometimes as big as small lakes (*étangs*). But if the soil has proved inadequate for productive farming it has yielded for centuries the basic materials of tile-making, pottery and some fine, distinctive *faïence*. Moving gradually southwards through the Nivernais with its expanses of forests and farms, then south-east through the Bazois and on to the Charolais, the land becomes noticeably more fertile, broken substantially only by the seams of coal and iron ore running south from Le Creusot through Montceau-les-Mines, which for centuries provided all that was necessary for an important and productive industrial area. (While most of the mines and forges are now closed, or survive only as museums, pockets of modern industrial development still benefit from the area's natural resources and contribute in an important way to the regional and indeed the national economy.) But even all these divisions will not satisfy all local people who not infrequently distinguish between the upper (*haut*) and lower (*bas*) part of their region as though speaking of different countries.

The Morvan is Burgundy's most forested area, but Burgundy itself is more heavily forested than any other region of France, and no-one can visit the region without being aware of the importance of wood. Burgundy's oaks, chestnuts, beeches, birches, poplars, elms and, more recently, pines have for ten centuries fired forges, produced charcoal and fuel, and provided building materials for all of France. Historical accounts tell how great rafts of logs were floated on the Yonne to Paris or the Saône to Lyon, and the *flotteurs* formed a society apart with their own traditions and values. Modernization in terms of transport or alternative materials brought the practice to an end by the early twentieth century but wood or logs remain somehow deeply part of the Burgundians' culture. Suddenly around a bend on a forest road you will be confronted by a great stack of logs, all beautifully cut and marked, stretching for 100 metres or more. And, on a more domestic scale, individual houses will have their piles of wood, carefully graded and replenished ready for winter. Burgundian winters can be severe, and it is easy to understand the importance of wood as fuel, but there is a respect for trees and wood, almost religious or cult-like, which is peculiarly Burgundian.

Access to Burgundy is easy. By express train from Paris (TGV) you can be there in two hours. By road, also from Paris, the A6 motorway cuts diagonally across towards Dijon before turning south via Beaune and Mâcon. From the north of France the A26 via Rheims offers an alternative. The national N7 road follows the Loire; the N6 shadows the A6 but is altogether more leisurely. Only if you wish to cross Burgundy from west to east is there a problem – at least if you are in a hurry. The sole major way is by the D978 from Nevers to Autun and thereafter the N80 to Mâcon. The reason for this, of course, is the great granite plateau of the Morvan, set almost exactly at the heart of Burgundy, but once inside the region speed is in any case the least of your concerns. As in so many areas of France, as soon as you are away from the main roads the ideal way to explore is to allow yourself to be drawn down tiny *routes communales* or *routes vicinales* (marked C and V on detailed maps) or even along tracks. There are also a good number of the long-distance hiking routes of the extensive national system, the Sentiers de Grande Randonnée, well signposted and with convenient overnight stopping places which allow access to even more remote areas. Exploration on horseback or even by bicycle is also possible and increasingly popular. Nor of course should the navigable rivers and canals, of which there are well over 1000 kilometres, be forgotten. With the decline in the use of Burgundy's waterways for commercial purposes, a leisure and tourist trade has developed and there are few more seductive sights than a brightly painted barge sailing gently between rows of majestic poplars on a hot summer's day, with drinks cooling in the ice-box, bicycles at the ready for a quick ride to the nearest baker's and the table set for a leisurely evening meal. But be warned: though they are great fun, barge holidays demand a lot of hard work and concentration, are distinctly less than pleasant in poor weather and are not cheap.

Wherever you go in Burgundy, and by whatever means, the legacies of a rich history are rarely far away. As a duchy or a state in its own right Burgundy reached its peak during the fourteenth and fifteenth centuries under the great Valois dukes, whose capital was Dijon. By all accounts theirs was an age when military might, political cunning and cultural wealth combined to create a dynastic empire rarely equalled in modern Europe. During this period Burgundy was quite separate from France and historical accounts detail the various treaties and deals made, notably with the English, as they engaged in a struggle for power. But there was little stability. Only when the last of the Valois dukes, Charles le Téméraire, was killed (along with 8000 Burgundian soldiers, it is said) in a battle with the Germans in 1477 and left no male heir did the king of France, Louis XI, seize as much of Burgundy as his armies could occupy, effectively bringing the duchy under French control.

Most authorities are agreed that the Burgundians first came from an island off the south coast of Sweden called Burgundarholm, moving south into central Europe as the power and influence of the Roman Empire began to decline in the fifth century. When they arrived they would have found the descendants of prehistoric man, Etruscans, Greeks, Gauls and Romans. Well-organized, reliable and adaptable, they blended easily with the local population, eventually imposing their rule, but by the early sixth century they were in conflict with the Franks from the east and were decisively defeated by them near Autun in 534, the year commonly accepted as marking the end of Burgundia, as it had been known for only about thirty years! But the name itself stuck and thereafter, until the emergence of the Valois dukes, Burgundy was part of the early power struggle involving the Franks, the Saracens from Spain, the Norse, the Gauls and the tribes from eastern Europe which would lead eventually to modern France. Yet Burgundy, like Provence, always retained a degree of independence and resisted attempts to centralize power and policy-making in Paris, however powerful the king. This may in part explain why parts of Burgundy suffered less, relatively speaking, than other regions of France at the time of the Revolution, though the damage done to some châteaux and churches was bad enough. This spirit of independence also had a more recent manifestation in the activities of the Resistance against the Nazi occupation of France between 1940 and 1944. Throughout the area simple memorials bear witness to the courage of those who fought to free France from fascism, and at Saint-Brisson in the Morvan there is a Musée de la Résistance which is arguably the best in the country.

Also fundamental to Burgundy's history is its role as a centre of Christianity. Its position as a natural crossroads brought missionaries, priests and pilgrims, and by the eleventh century Cluny had been established as the hub of a growing ecclesiastical empire independent of political control with its own characteristic Romanesque churches. When the world did not come to an end as expected in 1000, monasteries and their dependent institutions burgeoned, and by the early twelfth century there were 1450 of them with more than 10,000 monks spread across western Europe.

No account of Burgundy's ecclesiastical significance is complete without reference to Saint Bernard, born near Dijon in 1121. As an adolescent already committed to the monastery at Cîteaux, Bernard gradually turned against what he considered to be the laxity of Cluniac teaching and preached a new, austere and severe religion. But he was no mystic. Bernard emerged as a man of immense influence and a militant Christian who, inspired, it is said, by the Virgin herself, preached the Crusades and whose legacy shows him to have been as astute a politician as he was philosopher and theologian. I have to confess that while I never cease to admire the balance and harmony of Romanesque architecture, my real preference is for the plainest, unadorned style which Bernard advocated. While I am sure the loss is mine, I have always found it difficult to imagine how churches six or seven hundred years ago would have been illustrated with paintings and frescoes. I also prefer the plain style to the decorated polychrome tile roofs of so many Burgundian churches — and, indeed, of some secular buildings as well.

The general explanation offered for these multi-coloured roofs, found throughout the region, is that they are the continuation of a traditional style inherited from Flanders or from Austria. There is, however, a delightful and far more entertaining tale which forms part of Burgundian folk-lore. This tells how, in the Middle Ages, a rich Dijon merchant decided to have a new, sumptuous house built as a true indicator of his wealth. When only the tiling remained to be done he commissioned a highly talented local young man to do the work for him. However, the young *couvreur* was deeply in love with a girl named Viviane and spent his days staring in vain across the roofs at her window. Eventually she said she would only listen to his protestations of love if he did something extraordinary. By this time the merchant was beginning to get angry at his roof's not being tiled. Suddenly the young man had a flash of inspiration. He took hundreds of red and yellow tiles to the roof and worked non stop for two days. As he finished Viviane opened her window and saw written across the merchant's roof in huge letters: VIVE VIVIANE. Overcome, she at once accepted the young man's affections. But the merchant, while pleased enough by the tiler's work, had a wife whose name was other than Viviane and he therefore thought it politic to have the pattern modified. This the young man did, and with such success that his work was instantly in high demand and widely copied. He became rich and a unique feature of Burgundian building traditions was established.

This is just one of the many tales and legends for which Burgundy is renowned and I refer to others — the architect's owl on the church of Notre-Dame in Dijon, or the dragon guarding the hidden treasure on Mont Beuvray, for example — in the appropriate chapters.

I started this Introduction with wine, and I cannot finish it without some mention of food. Burgundian cuisine has achieved an international reputation and certainly some of the world's great chefs and their restaurants are to be found here. But not all sauce-rich dishes and heavy stews are truly Burgundian, whatever menus elsewhere may claim. Certain dishes, though, taste as they should only here: *oeufs en meurette*, eggs poached in red wine and onions; *râble de lièvre*, saddle of hare cooked either in mustard or with *marc de bourgogne*, a distilled wine spirit; various sausages or smoked hams and, nowadays, snails. These were once a peasant dish but the addition of garlic-rich sauces has made them into a gourmet's delight. It is not one I share with any enthusiasm, though I have friends who will drop everything once rain has brought out the snails and are not content until they have buckets full of the creatures being washed clean in brine. I talk about a number of different Burgundian dishes in the following pages as well as of the annual gastronomic fair held in Dijon every November which attracts people from all over France.

All of this and much more awaits the visitor to Burgundy. It is a region rich in unexpected delights which go far beyond those promised by the travel brochure and tourist office. Do not, however, expect an instant and unconditional welcome. Burgundy is one of the regions of France which has witnessed a slow but steady erosion of its population, with the houses left empty as a result bought by Parisians (for whom the journey from the capital is only two to three hours) or others, and local people are cautious. They may also seem taciturn, aloof and humourless at first. But Burgundian hospitality and friendship, once offered, is to be savoured. As my own acquaintance with the region grows so does my appreciation. Two experiences, one repeated often, crystallize much that is unique here. The first is of sitting on a train to Dijon at the height of autumn when the trees were full of the most striking reds and browns and oranges, prompting a little boy sitting behind me to say to his mother, 'Look, all those trees are burning.' The second, of which I never tire, is the sight of a buzzard hovering before it drops on some small unsuspecting mammal, or sitting motionless on a fence post, secure in its knowledge that it belongs to a region of which perhaps it alone has the secret.

1
The Northern Approaches

As I have already suggested, the northern edge of Burgundy is difficult to define with any precision, though access to the region is easy. Within an hour or so from Paris on the A6 motorway you pass a sign announcing '*Vous êtes en Bourgogne*' and the road conveniently slices across the region diagonally, allowing you to explore to the west or to the east, or it takes you directly to Beaune and to the heart of the wine country. Equally you can take either the N7 through Nemours down the western side, to join the Loire just north of Cosne and continue through La Charité and Nevers, or the N6 through Sens and thereafter the D905 to Tonnerre and the northeastern corner. But whichever route you choose there are few signs in the landscape to suggest that an immediate transition has been made from the Île de France or from Champagne; vast areas of flat agricultural land or of gently undulating woodland broken by farmsteads and tiny communities fill the horizon. But Burgundy it is. Churches, châteaux, even village houses begin almost imperceptibly to take on a different character. You have the sense not necessarily of moving into a more southern clime but of having begun to escape from the centralizing pull of Paris to penetrate one of France's greatest provinces.

If you arrive by the northernmost tip along the valley of the Yonne the cathedral tower at Sens soon beckons. To the south of the river a network of minor roads takes you through attractive woodland rising up from the valley and dotted with small villages, like Nailly, Saint-Serotin or Lixy with interesting churches parts of which date from the thirteenth and fourteenth centuries. Of them all the most interesting is Pont-sur-Yonne, where the vaulting in the twelfth-century Église de l'Assomption clearly anticipates similar work in the cathedral. Throughout its history Pont-sur-Yonne has been a strategic crossing point and, like Villeneuve-l'Archevêque to the east, a frontier town between regions. Caesar fought here against the Gauls, the English occupied the town in the fifteenth century, the Huguenots massacred the local population a hundred years later, the town was severely bombed in 1940. Rather more peaceably, Napoleon stayed here on his way to Paris in 1814. All signs of the early medieval bridge have gone and only a small section of its seventeenth-century successor is to be seen, now dwarfed and obscured by an ugly metal construction. Parts of the fortifications remain, together with a handful of medieval houses of which an old posting inn in the Rue de la Poste deserves to be seen. The Yonne is wide enough here for there to be no need of a canal and it is frequently busy with commercial and leisure traffic alike.

If you cross it and cut east through Gisy and follow the wooded valley of the Oreuse you arrive at Fleurigny on the edge of the Forêt de Launay, which with its sandy soil and sudden outcrops of large boulders is similar to the Forêt de Fontainebleau away to the west. On the outskirts of the village is an elegant château now restored after damage caused by the Germans during the Occupation. The present building, on the site of an older château, dates essentially from the sixteenth century. It is approached by way of a long, wooded drive which passes through a gatehouse constructed in 1840 from materials recuperated from the nearby village of Saint-Martin where there had been an important community of the Knights of Saint John. That so much of the château has survived is due in no small measure to the astuteness of the Marquis de Reaulx, father-in-law of the young widow of the Marquis de Fleurigny to whom the château belonged in the late eighteenth century. Fearing for her safety in the years immediately after the Revolution, she fled with her two young children to England, leaving her father-in-law in charge. Aware that the château could be severely damaged if not demolished by the revolutionaries, Reaulx repudiated his daughter's royalist sympathies, declared himself loyal to the new régime and obtained a passport for England. The château was safe and he returned several years later with his grandchildren to take up residence once again.

The château is surrounded by a moat which, with the north-facing façade and round towers, reminds us of its original military purpose even though some later elegant windows now break up the severity. The inner courtyard gives a quite different impression, however. Brick replaces stone and an arcade on the south side looks over a graceful lawn. Several of the rooms have been tastefully restored, notably the *salle des gardes*, with a massive carved fireplace depicting some remarkably aggressive boars, and a bedroom with early seventeenth-century wall paintings of hunting scenes and stories from mythology. But the 'gem' of the château, as it is called, is the chapel, in which much of the work is due to the talented Jean Cousin the Elder (c. 1490–1560), whom we will meet in Sens. The vaulted roof is always, and with justification, pointed out. No fewer than forty bosses decorate it, bearing hanging designs in the forms of flowers, leaves and birds. The richly coloured window depicting the classical story of the 'Sybille de Tibur', who points dramatically at Mary and the Infant Jesus enthroned in clouds, is also impressive and much admired. The château has remained in the hands of the same family (sometimes rather distant members) until the present day and is open to the public. On the last Sunday of July the whole village and many others from the region gather here to celebrate the annual *kermesse*, a village fête, sometimes focussing on a grand meal and at which local goods and produce are sold in aid of charity.

From Fleurigny and nearby Thorigny the main road climbs up quite steeply through the forest before dropping down through Soucy to Sens. But to sweep round south-east to Villeneuve-l'Archevêque opens up an attractive wedge of countryside with pockets of dense woodland and unexpected panoramic views over the nearby city. The Grande Randonnée 2 also links Fleurigny with Villeneuve and another popular and much publicized way of exploring the region is on horseback.

On the border between Burgundy and Champagne, Villeneuve-l'Archevêque owes its name to having been the property of the archbishops of Sens up to the time of the Revolution. It has retained its medieval street pattern and around the north doorway of the thirteenth-century church of Notre-Dame are a number of carvings, notably of the Annunciation and of Saint Anne, mercifully spared mutilation at the hands of Revolutionary zealots. Inside the church, a depiction of the Holy Sepulchre with not only Mary, John and Mary Magdelene but two embalmers ready with their jars of oil is strikingly realistic. Villeneuve's most celebrated feature, however, is the section of the Aqueduc de la Vanne, originally constructed by the Romans to take water to Sens. As Paris began to grow in the nineteenth century and a bigger water supply became necessary, many of the water-mills and springs outside the city came under compulsory purchase. The aqueduct was extended east into the Aube and north to Paris and while in places it is architecturally impressive it has sorely reduced the amount of water in the Vanne. Nowhere is this more striking and unfortunate than in the grounds of the former château, now a hospital. Local people, not surprisingly, remain angry.

Sens

Situated on the confluence of the Vanne and the Yonne, Sens seems in atmosphere to belong as much to the Île de France as to Burgundy. More than any of the other local communities it was for centuries a frontier town and a focal point for tradespeople, and there is no better day to visit Sens and experience this than a Monday, when the square in front of the cathedral and the narrow surrounding streets become one large market.

The city owes its name to the Senons, the Gaulish people who inhabited the region before the Roman conquest. Renamed Agendicum by the Romans, it developed into an important trading, administrative and military centre, and while relatively little evidence of its full size remains it is certain that it extended beyond the irregularly shaped oval area marked out by the *boulevards*, or *promenades* as they are known locally. According to legend Saint Peter himself sent Saint Savinien to evangelize the area, though it is now known that Christianity did not arrive here for another 300 years. In 1163-4 Pope Alexander III stayed in Sens and, until Paris became an archbishopric in 1627, the city remained the most significant centre of medieval Christendom in this part of France, with its jurisdiction spreading across Burgundy as far as Nevers.

So well protected was Sens by its fortifications that it successfully resisted various attacks, notably from the Moslems in 731 and from the Normans in 886. By the twelfth and thirteenth centuries it had reached the height of its importance, a fact recognized most clearly perhaps in 1234 by the celebration in its cathedral of the marriage of Louis XI to Marguerite de Provence. But during the late Middle Ages Sens suffered; it was occupied by English troops in 1420 and seriously damaged during the Wars of Religion. Revolutionary troops, too, destroyed much in 1793 and when, early in the nineteenth century, the first *départements* were created, Sens was passed over as the capital of the Yonne in favour of Auxerre – a slight from which its inhabitants have never fully recovered. This loss of status was symbolically underlined in the mid nineteenth century by the demolition of the city's walls.

No matter from which direction you approach Sens, the cathedral of Saint-Étienne dominates the skyline. Begun around the mid twelfth century on the initiative of the archbishop Henri Sanglier, who was a friend of Saint Bernard, it is the oldest of France's Gothic cathedrals. Architecturally it offers its visitors a complete range of styles from the immediate post-Romanesque to the most flamboyant Late Gothic elegance of the late sixteenth century. The architect Guillaume de Sens took it as a model for his reconstruction of the choir of Canterbury Cathedral around 1180 and a statue of Thomas Becket, that 'turbulent priest' who spent four years at Sens, stands on the north side of the church just after the crossing.

The most impressive feature of the outside is without doubt the west façade, despite the immense damage caused by the Revolutionary forces on their way north from Marseille in 1793. The oldest part is the north tower, known as the Tour de Plomb on account of a lead-covered belfry with which it was capped until the mid nineteenth century. Its companion tower (Tour de

Pierre) collapsed at the end of the thirteenth century and was rebuilt 300 years later. With its campanile it is nearly 80 metres high. The combined weight of its two sixteenth-century bells (La Savinienne and La Potentienne) is 3000 kilograms! Fortunately they survived the Revolution when other bells were melted down and transformed into cannons. Of the various carvings and statuaries which remain — and erosion caused by pollution is an ongoing problem — particular notice should be paid to the bestiary representing either certain characteristics (the ass symbolizes ignorance, for example) or different parts of the world: a camel represents Arabia, an elephant India and so on. Between the doors of the central arch is a statue of Saint Étienne himself, fortunately spared by the Revolutionaries who, it is said, decorated his head with a Phrygian cap!

If the outside of the cathedral appears rather varied, the interior is remarkable for its balance and proportion. The roof of the nave is low but instead of seeming to crush or overpower gives an impression of solidity, reinforced by the alternating heavy pillars and pairs of slim columns. Over the centuries the fairly austere quality of the original church has been modified by alterations to the windows which allowed more light into the building, and by the addition of the transept at the very end of the fifteenth century and of various chapels. But fundamental to the balance within Saint-Étienne is the Cistercian belief that the perfection and harmony of God's creation could be reflected in mathematical balance and precision. As a result you find architectural features — rows of arches, pillars or windows for example — based on pure numbers such as three or seven, or being proportionately in relation to each other. Thus eight stout pillars would carry eight more slender ones which in turn would rise into twelve. (Saint-Étienne contains some examples but better ones will be found in the great monastery at Fontenay and in particular at Vézelay.) There are also more intimate details to be admired here on capitals and at the bases of pillars — carvings of beasts, monsters, rustic scenes or simple designs. And the stained glass is impressive. The southern windows, which depict among other things the Tree of Jesse, the Annunciation and the story of Saint Nicholas (the work of sixteenth-century craftsmen from

Troyes), and those in the choir devoted to Becket's life have to be seen in bright sunlight for the richness of the blues and reds to be fully appreciated. Other features of note are the wrought-iron gates to the choir, the group of stucco figures by Joseph Hermand representing the martyrdom of Saint Savinien, the first bishop of Sens, and the unusual sixteenth-century monument erected by Tristan de Salazar to the memory of his parents. His father is depicted as kneeling on a slab supported by four black marble columns. The figure of his mother was destroyed during the Revolution, as was the altar, also in black marble, which they would have been facing. Finally, the cathedral treasure should not be missed. Still one of the richest in France, it must have been quite sumptuous before most of its gold and silver objects were carted away at the end of the eighteenth century. On display are ivory boxes and carvings from the fifth and sixth centuries, enamelled ornaments, religious robes (including one belonging to Becket, for example), tapestries, illustrated manuscripts and pieces of shrouds including the one used to wrap the body of Saint Victor. Charlemagne is said to have bequeathed the jewels and relics to Sens from his own chapel.

To the south of Saint-Étienne is a courtyard, once the Archbishops' garden. It is surrounded by buildings, one of which is the town museum which acts as a focal exhibition centre for the whole region and where a large and varied collection charts the evolution of man's presence in the valley of the Yonne from prehistory through to Roman times. One especially fine exhibit is a huge, brightly coloured mosaic which depicts the sun god Apollo in his chariot. But the most important part of these buildings is the thirteenth-century episcopal palace on the west side, whose original upper floor was destroyed when the tower collapsed in 1268. Half religious and half secular, the building is intriguing. On the ground floor are the cells, untouched for 600 years, their walls still bearing inscriptions and pictures carved by prisoners. Many are religious in inspiration, exclamations of repentance or appeals to God; one, less clear, depicts a priest who is either releasing prisoners or putting them into chains and shackles. On the floor above is the *salle de réunion*, a room of some style as befits the meetings and receptions which took place there and still do. In past winters it must have been bitterly cold, especially for those sitting on the stone benches around the walls – the huge fireplace would have ensured at least some warmth, if only for the most important dignitaries. On the southern side of the square and leading into the Rue des Déportés is the Passage de Moïse. The door on the street side, in a severe, defensive wall, bears a carving of Saint Étienne's martyrdom. Just inside this door a stairway leads to the eastern wing where the episcopal rooms have been restored and where the original servants' quarters in the attics are now a picture gallery.

While from a distance Saint-Étienne dominates Sens, within the town it seems to be much more tightly integrated than the cathedrals of Auxerre or Nevers, for example. It is virtually at the central point of medieval Sens and little has been done over the centuries to open up an area around it. In fact, rather the opposite has happened. Restoration of houses and streets has been careful. In both the Grande Rue, the main east–west axis of Sens, and in the Rue de la République which crosses it at right angles just in front of the cathedral, there are a number of fifteenth- and sixteenth-century, half-timbered houses which now bear plaques indicating, where they are known, the names and occupations of their original owners. The most impressive of these is undoubtedly the Maison d'Abraham in the Rue de la République which belonged to a leather worker whose tools are depicted on one of the main corner posts. The same house also has an impressive carving of the Tree of Jesse with the seven Kings of Israel and culminating in an image of the Virgin Mary carrying the infant Jesus. Several other houses in adjacent streets were occupied by various religious orders – Jesuits, Carmelites, Ursulines for example – a reminder of Sens' importance as a spiritual centre up to the end of the eighteenth century.

Once you have wandered the patchwork of the narrow central medieval streets, the outer *boulevards* offer a pleasant walk around the town in about an hour. From the southern end of the Rue de la République you turn left into the Boulevard du 14 Juillet, where the only substantial section of the original fortifications has been preserved. East and past the site of the gateway on the road to Troyes is the Place des Héros and a memorial to those who were killed in the Franco-Prussian war of 1870–71, and just off this square a passage leads to the Gué Saint-Jean, the *lavoir*, or public wash-house, and the Mondereau stream which in the Middle Ages flowed into the ditches outside the town walls. Round to the north side along the Boulevard du Mail, across the Place Jean-Jaurès and past the one-time Porte de Paris is a large, unattractive, but on market-days essential area for car parking and the site of a semi-permanent fairground. After this you come round to the west side of the town and the river, popular with tourists (especially with Germans) taking boating holidays and busy with commercial traffic. Once barges filled with huge tree trunks would have plied their way north past Pont-sur-Yonne to meet the Seine at Montereau, but now oil, bricks and tiles, and cereals are the most common cargo. There is also a bridge here, the Pont Lucien Cornet, across to the Île d'Yonne and the pretty twelfth-century church of Saint-Maurice sitting low down by the water's edge. Finally, along the southern edge of the town is the Cours Tarbé, completely taken over by stalls on market-days, and some pleasant public gardens with a statue of Jean Cousin the Elder, the designer, painter, sculptor and glassmaker whose work can be admired in the cathedral and was seen in the chapel at Fleurigny.

South from Sens the N6 follows the wooded valley of the Yonne to Joigny and after Villeneuve-sur-Yonne provides one of the most attractive sections of any major national road in this part of France. As you approach Villeneuve the village, now bypassed, slopes gently down to the river tightly clustered around the church of Notre-Dame. The main street is only about 400 metres long and has a fortified gate, dating from the thirteenth century, at each end – only these two remain of the original five. The flinty soil in the area encouraged human settlement from the earliest times, yet, rather oddly, neither the Gauls nor the Romans attempted to establish a permanent community here. In fact, the Roman road from Auxerre to Sens was on the opposite bank, its line partly followed today by the departmental one. But people later had different ideas. In 1163 Louis VII decided to develop a town here and during the Middle Ages Villeneuve enjoyed strategic and commercial importance. Disaster struck in 1594 during the Wars of Religion when it was sacked and largely destroyed by fire, but undeterred the citizens set about rebuilding their town and prosperity came again, particularly with an important river trade in wood, wine, coal and leather. With the changing modes of transport and the phylloxera crisis some of this was lost, but recent years have witnessed, as at Avallon, the development of a small light-industrial estate. This and, more significantly, the exploitation of the river for tourism have ensured relative prosperity again. Villeneuve also has a thriving antiques trade and every year an important and popular fair is held at Whitsun.

Two and a half centuries ago this must have been a pleasing and elegant place. The façades of many of the seventeenth- and eighteenth-century houses in the main street, the Rue Carnot, have been tastefully restored. Of particular note are the Hôtel du Dauphin and the Maison des Sept Têtes, almost opposite the church and so called on account of the mythological figures carved on its front. Of note for a different reason is the Hôtel Régence which in the late 1920s was owned by Villeneuve's mayor, Dr Marcel Petiot. He left for Paris in 1932 where ten years later during the Occupation he befriended a series of Jews, promising them medical help only to murder them. He was tried and executed in 1946 but there has always remained in some people's minds the view that Petiot was a scapegoat and executed for reasons of political expediency.

From either end of the Rue Carnot you can walk round the line of the 2 kilometres of medieval fortifications. Some of these have been attractively incorporated into private gardens and in the north-eastern corner of the village is a solid-looking tower, the original keep of the thirteenth-century château. Old drawings show it to be considerably higher than it is today but what is left, with walls 4 metres thick, looks indestructible. Of the two remaining gates, the Porte de Joigny to the south has been turned into a small museum and an exhibition centre where there is a particularly fine sixteenth-century drawing on parchment by Jean Chéreau of the west front of Notre-Dame. Outside the tower and under the stone bridge over the original ditch is a splendid vaulted *lavoir*, still regularly in use.

Without question the main building of interest in Villeneuve is the church. Unfortunately it is frequently locked but the key can usually be obtained from the presbytery in the Rue Pierrot. Begun in the thirteenth century and built over 300 years, it has features of both Burgundian and Champagne architecture. But it is a surprisingly uniform building and inside offers a delicacy (more Gothic than Romanesque) and luminosity which I find more striking than in Saint-Étienne in Sens. Several of the chapels are of note, among them the Chapelle des Mariniers, appropriately dedicated to Saint Nicholas and with paintings depicting episodes from his life, or the first chapel on the south side illustrating the life of the Virgin Mary. On the other side of the nave is a representation of Christ's entombment. The figures (attributed to Jean Goujon (c. 1510–68), whose skill can be admired in many of the figures decorating the Louvre) are of stone, except for that of Christ which, though of unknown origin, is at least 200 years older and carved from limewood. Also of interest is the macabre funerary slab, now plastered into the church wall, of a priest named Dubourg. His body is depicted semi-clad and being eaten by worms.

With the oak and beech trees of the Forêt de la Briffe and the Forêt du Pavillon Gros rising to the east, the road closely follows the meanderings of the Yonne to Joigny. About half-way and set deep in these woods is the Château de Palteau, beautifully restored in the 1950s and now a *colonie de vacances*, much frequented by groups of chattering children. From here you can take a section of the Grande Randonnée 213 across the forests to the Côte-Saint-Jacques on the edge of Joigny.

Joigny

Although well under half the size of Sens and only a quarter that of Auxerre, just 30 kilometres to the south, Joigny is nonetheless very much a frontier town. Situated on a spur of high ground on the east bank of the Yonne, it looks south towards central Burgundy, to which it truly belongs, and north towards Champagne under whose tutelage it was for long periods in the Middle Ages. To the east are the pleasant, undulating expanses of oak, beech and birch trees of the Forêt d'Othe which once spread uninterrupted to the departmental boundary 35 kilometres away. Now it is divided up by patches of farmed land and also contains an area for the military to carry out exercises. To the west a countryside largely dominated by agriculture disappears in the direction of the Gâtinais and the western edge of Burgundy.

A Gallo-Roman settlement known as Joviniacum existed here and, at the end of the tenth century, Rainard le Vieux built the first castle and fortifications, remnants of which can be seen today in the Porte de Saint-Jean in the centre of town and along the Rue des Fosses. Two hundred years later the town had grown and on the steeper eastern side the line of the walls followed the Rue de la Guimbarde. One of the gates from this later period, the Porte de Bois with its dumpy round towers, can be seen on the north side just opposite the main cemetery. During the Middle Ages Joigny developed a flourishing cloth trade and while a severe fire in July 1530 destroyed much, rebuilding in the following hundred years and careful modern restoration mean that the elegance and prosperity of that period can still be appreciated. A number of buildings have the characteristic deep, often double cellars of which there are good examples in Nevers as well. In these much of the wine for which Joigny was also renowned was stored; today, though diminished, the reputation remains, especially for *vin gris*, a special form of rosé wine made from black grapes whose skins are removed immediately after pressing.

At the highest point of the town is the Église de Saint-Jean, one of three important churches and built on the site of a tenth-century monastery. None of them is particularly striking though each has various features which deserve to be seen. The display of ornate panelling in the nave roof of Saint-Jean is justifiably much admired and two tombs are of particular note. The first is a white marble representation of Christ in the Holy Sepulchre surrounded by seven mourning figures including Mary and the disciples. This was carved by Mathieu Laigniel around 1520 for the funerary chapel of the Lannoy family and was brought to Joigny from Folleville in the Somme by Pierre de Gondi, whose family established themselves here in the sixteenth century. The second is the tomb of Adélaïs de Joigny, who died in 1187, which was transferred from the one-time abbey at Dilo in the Forêt d'Othe. At the head of the stone figure is the curious carving of a laughing young man in a tree, eating a cake. Unbeknown to him two creatures are gnawing through the branch on which he is sitting. The symbolism of death's being present even in our most carefree moments is not as grim or as obvious here as it is in the *danse macabre* to be seen in the church at nearby Ferté-Loupière to the south-west; the carving might even be thought to suggest encouragement to enjoy life while there is time. But death is there none the less. Whether or not the carving of Adélaïs is a true representation remains a mystery.

The other two churches are smaller. In the eastern area of the town, once the centre of the wine trade, is Saint-André, reconstructed between the fourteenth and sixteenth centuries on the site of an eleventh-century church. Around the main door the only decoration to have withstood vandalism and erosion by the weather is, appropriately, of vines. Inside is a length of ladder, said to have been used by the English during the unsuccessful siege of Joigny in 1429. Saint-Thibault, to the west and outside the medieval walls, was also badly damaged by the fire of 1530. Its patron saint, who in his early years and before his conversion at the age of 24 enjoyed the life of a young squire, is depicted in a panel above the north door. He is on a rearing horse and is dressed in a flowing cloak, ready for a fast ride or a hunting expedition. Inside the church opposite the pulpit is an elegant, beautifully proportioned statue of the Virgin Mary, holding the infant Jesus who is reaching up with his left hand to touch his mother's cheek. Attention is customarily drawn to the 'Vierge au Sourire', as this statue is known, on account of the carved folds of Mary's clothes; it is infinitely more moving, in my view, for the gestures and expression of shared affection between a mother and her child, free from the overtones of Christ's divinity so typical of much church art of the fourteenth century.

The top of the rise around Saint-Jean is easily reached by the road which leads up from the river, passing through a pedestrian area busy with local people most of the time, but especially so on Saturday mornings, when people from surrounding villages come for the market, and at the time of Joigny's two most celebrated fairs – the one held over Easter weekend and the other, specializing in melons and onions, on 14 September. Just to the right, the Rues Haute and Basse Pêcherie are reminders of the role fishing has played in local trade and cuisine. From here through a network of narrow side-streets you emerge in the Place

Saint-Jean by the church, with the substantial remains of the Gondi château and the restored gateway. West through this takes you into an area not only much destroyed in 1530 but also badly damaged in bombing raids in 1940 and much more recently by a gas explosion in 1981. Restorative work has been particularly successful here, however, and of Joigny's many medieval houses the three outstanding examples are all within a few hundred metres of one another. First is the Maison du Bailly in the Rue Montant-au-Palais, an impressive building clearly once the property of a rich family, on three floors with different styles of cross-timbering and with carvings on the corner posts. Second is the Maison de l'Arbre de Jessé, just beyond, with the biblical story carved quite clearly. Third is the Maison du Pilori, dating from the sixteenth century with some grotesque heads of monsters and rather more sedate statuettes of the saints Francis, John the Baptist and Martin. Beyond these the Rue Davier brings you to the outer *boulevards*. Modern Joigny has expanded but it is easy to walk round the town as it existed until the early years of the twentieth century well within two hours by following these and then the *quais*.

Should you have occasion to talk to local people you may be struck by their humour. Like their Burgundian cousins from further south they are also said to be fiercely independent and it is likely too, if history is any indication, that they do not suffer authoritarian behaviour lightly. In 1438 the overlord of Joigny, the Comte Guy de Trémoille, attempted to impose his will and demand tributes from his people to a degree they thought was excessive. They attacked the château, seized the count and unceremoniously battered him to death with the mallets used for knocking bungs into barrels of wine. To this day the town's coat of arms bears the mallet as one of its symbols and Joigny people, or Joviniens, are still nicknamed Maillotins. Whether these things refer to that incident long ago or merely reflect the importance of wine for the town's economy over the years, however, must remain a matter for speculation.

If, instead of plunging straight down the valley of the Yonne, you approach Burgundy in a more leisurely way from the north-west, Montargis is a delightful introduction. Although in character and atmosphere it belongs to Burgundy, the town is, of course, in the Loiret department and, even more importantly for local people, in the Gâtinais to which, if pressed, they will claim allegiance rather than to Burgundy as a whole. For them this larger area does not begin until you reach Courtenay, about 20 kilometres to the east where the terrain develops a number of shallow valleys. The distinction is a nice one, however, a reflection more of a sense of local allegiance than any serious wider view. In their economic dependence on water and forests the Montargois are in the same position as most of their fellow Burgundians 30 kilometres or so further south in the Puisaye or the western stretches of the Nivernais. It should also be said that in the late twentieth century Montargis is in a kind of limbo. Already it is comfortably within two hours of Paris, but the promised extension of the motorway system and of the TGV during the next decade will bring it easily within daily commuting distance of the capital and link it in the opposite direction with Orléans to the south-west. Together, these developments could well have the effect of pulling it away from Burgundy, and that would be a pity.

At present with its principal suburb of Amilly, Montargis is a sprawling place cut by the river Loing and by three canals, the Loing, Briare and Orléans, with their many tributaries and links. This presence of water brings coolness in summer but at other times can make the air quite raw. A most agreeable way to begin a visit is to follow the tow-path of the Briare east from the north side of the town, passing the ornate nineteenth-century town hall and its rather fine gardens (Jardin Durzy) until you reach a double lock and an extraordinarily steep, stepped iron bridge. Across this is the Boulevard Belles-Manières, following the line of the town's sixteenth-century fortifications which today form the foundations of a line of substantial houses. Thereafter the centre is so small that you can wander at will using the 126 bridges to enjoy the waterways with their washhouses, ramshackle balconies festooned with hanging baskets of flowers in summer, and the occasional optimistic fisherman. In several places houses have been modernized and altered, but a number have retained the original brick walls strapped with oak beams. An excellent illustration of what has been achieved is in the north-west corner of the town, near the junction of the Canal de Briare and the Loing, where a Gâtinais museum has been created. Here you will discover the complete side of a house with its connecting galleries and outside stairway, and it is easy to imagine the kind of enclosed communities these places once housed not all that long ago. No one should leave Montargis either before sampling the local pralines. These grilled almonds coated in rough sugar were invented here in the seventeenth century by one of the Duc de Plessis-Praslin's cooks and have earned Montargis a unique reputation in France ever since, though I have to confess that they are not to my taste.

If you leave Montargis to the south, remaining for a while in the Loiret, you follow the neat valley of the Briare and Loing. Half-way between Montcresson and Châtillon-Coligny are the remains of a small Gallo-Roman amphitheatre, sadly neglected now and nothing like the one to be seen much further south at Autun, for example, but still a reminder of the civilization that was here centuries ago. A dozen kilometres further on is Châtillon, a convenient point at which to cut east to the border between the departments of the Loiret and Yonne. As at Montargis, water is much in evidence and the village is ringed by a small moat and parts of the twelfth-century fortifications. Just inside a gate on the south-western side, in the Rue de la Poterne, are some impressive sixteenth-century houses and the town's former prison. On the eastern side near the church is an interesting stone-built house, once the site of a salt vendor's with a high gable and trellised stairway. And as you leave by the D56 you pass the twelfth-century keep of the first château and a series of terraces dating from three centuries later. On one of these is an *orangerie* attributed to Jean Goujon, whose work is also on display in the church of Notre Dame at Villeneuve-sur-Yonne.

As you move south and east from Châtillon-Coligny the ground begins to rise gently but steadily as the Gâtinais gives way to the Puisaye, an extensive plateau stretching down into the northern ranges of the Nièvre and east to the Morvan. There are hundreds of *étangs*, some as big as small lakes, and dozens of streams. Patches of dark soil alternate with pockets of dense woods and expanses of dank, sour land dotted with clumps of coarse grass creating a landscape which the novelist Colette recalled as 'sad, darkened by forests . . . where even goats cannot live'. In parts inhospitable and even hostile, the area has, over the centuries, provided refuge for clandestine groups. The secretive meetings of the guild of charcoal makers, of Jansenist priests or of Resistance fighters have all left their mark. Legends too are rife. Stories of mysterious white figures, of werewolves, witches and soothsayers are still told, not without a certain degree of malicious pleasure, in particular to the Parisians who come in search of weekend and holiday homes. As in the far north-eastern corner of Burgundy around Châtillon-sur-Seine, living has never been easy here for local people. Apart from a reasonably successful trade in wood up to the nineteenth century, only the manufacture of bricks and tiles had much commercial success, though pottery-making has had a long and important tradition as artists worked the local clay to produce a ware (*grès*) which is distinctively brown or dark grey. The centre for this activity is Saint-Amand. Several families have worked here for generations and there are twenty or thirty potters whose studios are regularly open; invitations to inspect their work are as plentiful as they are between Dijon and Beaune to sample wine. Enthusiasm is high once you get people talking about their skills and the 'secrets' of their art: glazing, methods of painting and fixing of colours, even the choice of wood for firing certain kilns. And once you have shown a genuine interest you can reasonably expect to purchase a piece which if not a bargain will be of good quality. Also at Saint-Amand is the only national pottery school in France.

If you wander diagonally south-east across the Puisaye a number of villages deserve to be visited. First is Bléneau, in my experience not at all the 'cheerless place' it has been described as by one commentator. Bustling, smart and self-confident, Bléneau is ideally visited when the morning market is in full swing. The first time I came here I was looking for the château. A lady on her way to the market whom I asked for help looked at me with some astonishment since, as she said, there are several! Although she had lived here all her life the one I was after had, somewhat unusually, not made much of an impression. Perhaps there are reasons for this since, while clearly visible, the Château de Bléneau is quite definitely closed to the public. In style it is a mixture of a chunky medieval castle (rebuilt in the sixteenth century) and an elegant eighteenth-century house. In beautiful condition, it stands proudly surrounded by a wide moat and immaculately kept parkland. Its vegetable garden and tennis court suggest regular occupation: so do the large alsatian dogs running free just inside the ornate gates and railings.

A dozen kilometres beyond Bléneau along the valley of the Loing and across a countryside farmed for cereals, sugar beet and some soft fruit is Saint-Fargeau, dominated by its château whose role in village life is central. During the months of July and August on Friday nights there is a magnificent *son et lumière* spectacle illustrating the château's history. Established in 1980, this is justifiably considered to be one of the best in France; and if the expense involved is huge so is the revenue, vital for the refurbishment of the building. During these months the village's population trebles to around 6000, giving a much needed boost to the local economy. Until very recently the centre of a relatively poor agricultural region, Saint-Fargeau is about to enter an era of prosperity. The projected motorway will make the link with Paris easier, but investment in a factory specializing in metal constructions has already eased an unemployment problem. More significant still was the decision taken in 1991 to create a centre at Champcevrais, just north of Bléneau, for conferences and for retraining people in information technology. It is managed by the Club Méditerranée and will eventually attract up to 5000 people a year. With three golf courses and a full range of leisure activities this promises to be one of the biggest and most attractive ventures of its kind in this part of France. As one hotel manager said to me, if only one per cent of all those people were to decide at some point to return to Saint-Fargeau for a holiday it would be worth it.

Built of brick, with a slate roof and a central five-sided courtyard, the château is disconcertingly irregular in shape. The main door is reached by a drawbridge over the wide, deep ditches which, until the early nineteenth century, contained the moat. At each corner is a tower topped by a conical roof; all but one to the north, known as the Tour Jacques-Coeur (after the château's purchaser in the mid fifteenth century), are further decorated by quite fine lanterns. Virtually all of the existing building is in the style of the work of François le Vau, architect to Louis XIV, whose designs – which included the palace at Versailles – were much in vogue in the mid seventeenth century. Le Vau was commissioned by Anne-Marie-Louise d'Orléans, an enormously wealthy cousin of the king and better known by the name of Duchesse de Montpensier, whose unhappy love life was recounted by Madame de Lafayette. She came here during a period of civil disturbance between the king and some of his nobles known as the Fronde, and enjoyed a social life which saw her entertain on a lavish scale. When she first arrived – after a seven-day coach journey from the capital – it is said that knee-high grass and brambles filled the courtyard and that the walls and roof were crumbling. Le Vau took twenty years to restore the château completely, but his work was severely damaged by fire a hundred years later in 1752 and the château was not properly rebuilt until the early nineteenth century. Since the late 1960s it has been in private hands and the current owners have put up a small public notice just inside the main gate which is a salutary reminder of the enormous cost of maintaining a historic building of these dimensions: 'Each individual entrance fee pays for three slates.' Apart from that hard economic fact a visit is worthwhile. Though much of the restoration bears the rather pompous hallmarks of the nineteenth century, the *salle des gardes* with its fine beams and original floor, the Tour Jacques-Coeur and in particular the roof deserve close inspection. The last is literally hugely impressive. Massive oak beams originally soaked in the local *étang* and weighing over 1000 kilograms form a structure which often resembles the ribs of an upside down ship or of a giant's umbrella. Some of the key beams have pieces of string tied between them, a remarkably simple but, one hopes, totally effective way of checking on any significant movement.

Shortly after she had installed herself and her entourage at Saint-Fargeau, Mlle de Montpensier spent a few days at the nearby château of Ratilly. Used perhaps to the relative comfort of Saint-Fargeau (though it is hardly Versailles), she found her neighbours' home unbearably bleak and she quickly returned. Since then, but only in recent years, things have improved. In 1951 the château at Ratilly was purchased by Jeanne and Norbert Pierlot who established their internationally known pottery there. The tradition is carried on still by their daughter Nathalie.

The story of discovery of the château by the Pierlots is romantic. Jeanne (who died in 1988) tells, in a letter which the family still has, of how in January 1939 she went one day to Ratilly from Saint-Amand where she was an apprentice to Le Père Lion, whose studio can still be visited. 'On Friday we went to see the château de Ratilly just 12 kilometres away, a magnificent fortified château dating from the twelfth century surrounded by trees. We crossed the drawbridge and rang. After a long time a shutter creaked open and a voice cried out 'Who are you?' Then the window opened and the owner pushed her head out. She was an old woman, 82 years old, in her night-dress and wearing a dishevelled wig. She said she was ill and couldn't see anyone. She lives there entirely alone, does her own cooking or rather doesn't and lives on *croissants* which she buys once a fortnight.' Eventually, having borrowed money and having persuaded the local priest of their good intentions, the Pierlots became the proud owners of Ratilly a dozen years later.

You approach it down a small drive lined with neatly trimmed hedges, then across a fixed bridge to the main entrance. This has three floors, is topped by a slate-covered belfry and is flanked by two round towers which are integrated into the front façade. At each of the corners is a round tower; the south-west one contains the pigeon loft with over 200 nesting holes, and still has the original ladder, attached by a frame to a central pole, which sweeps round the walls enabling the eggs to be collected. With its mottled grey and ochre walls, its grass-covered courtyard ('*le grand carré*' as it is known), its trees and well, Ratilly is delightfully appealing during the summer and early autumn. But on a raw day in early spring or under snow it is easy to understand why Mlle de Montpensier left in such a hurry. Even after careful restoration the family's private rooms facing north remain relatively bleak. The only one I found comfortable is the tiny library in which the person cataloguing the château's small collection of books shuts herself away with a radiator full on. Even so for thirty years now Ratilly has drawn people to it during the summer months from all over the world. Exhibitions, courses in potting and classical music concerts are much sought after and popular, and people who have been privileged to live there for a short while talk enthusiastically of the warmth of the welcome they have received and of the genuine intellectual and emotional stimulus they have discovered. My own link with Ratilly is an average-sized jug of mat pale mauve with a speckled finish, made by Nathalie.

The southernmost tip of the Yonne is scattered with tiny hamlets, some dilapidated, some, like Vrille, bright and carefully restored. East from Ratilly is Perreuse and the source of the Loing, marked by a plaque set in brick by a small pond. The departmental road (D7) then leads north passing the château of L'Orme du Pont, most definitely shut to the public but standing in magnificent landscaped grounds. Beyond is Saint-Sauveur, with its fine seventeenth-century buildings grouped around the massive remains of a twelfth-century stone keep. They are now owned by the local council and extensively and successfully used for local festivities of all kinds. Saint-Sauveur is also the birthplace of Colette and in the street named after her is the substantial town house, now owned by a doctor, where she spent her childhood. Readers of *La Maison de Claudine* or *Sido* will find in them what is considered to be a realistic description of Saint-Sauveur in the late nineteenth century: it bears little resemblance to the present one.

East from Saint-Sauveur and Ratilly the landscape changes again, becoming drier, stonier and bare and scarred with quarries. The dark-coloured stone of houses in the Puisaye gives way to limestone, and small communities are replaced by larger centres of population. Of these arguably the most attractive is Druyes-les-Belles-Fontaines, hard up against a cliff face topped by the ruins of a twelfth-century castle. The best time to arrive is either with the evening sun setting on the castle or when mists are rising from the springs and source of the Druyes in the valley. A hundred cubic metres of water per second gush out − not in itself a huge amount, but the noise it makes as it surges under buildings and streets through a series of weirs and channels is amplified as it bounces off the cliff-face. And if water is everywhere so are the local ducks. Certainly, out of the tourist season at least, they seem more numerous than human beings and wander proprietorially through the streets, apparently oblivious to possible danger from an occasional car. The village is well kept. Its Romanesque church should be visited if only for its main entrance, as should the 1831 *lavoir* in the principal street with its intricate roof. To the west of the centre a path leads steeply up to the castle and to the original village which can also be approached from Courson through a fourteenth-century gate, all that remains of the original fortifications. The castle is in need of restoration and local activity to muster support is strong. With luck, and maybe with some state or departmental assistance, something will be achieved and this would be commendable since the building is a good example of the transition between a military château and an aristocratic dwelling. During the summer there is a small exhibition on life in Druyes over the centuries, and just outside the small tourist office is a rather sad oak tree which, it is claimed, was planted on 14 July 1789.

The journey from Druyes to Auxerre takes no more than three-quarters of an hour by the most direct route. A slower but more picturesque way is north through the edge of the Forêt de Frétoy to Taingy (at nearly 400 metres), then Leugny on the Ouanne and finally Toucy, to be visited on a Saturday when its market is in full swing. Its centre is the Place de la République with stalls clustered around the stern-looking bust of Pierre Larousse (1817–75), who was born here. During his lifetime he was celebrated for a number of grammar books and dictionaries, but his dream was to produce a book which would 'provide an answer to every question'. He died before this could be accomplished but, as every student of French knows, the groundwork at least was done. Toucy has other attractions too. A settlement was here from Gallo-Roman times and as its importance grew so did the need for security. Fortifications were begun in the tenth century and 300 years later the whole village was behind walls. Parts of these are still visible, especially around the church, whose apse looks more like part of a castle. This area of the town has some interesting medieval houses though they need attention. The Rue de l'Église and the Rue de la Motte leading off the main square are good examples, as is the tiny Passage du Chapeau Rouge which used to be guarded, it is said (and may still be) by a dog called, appropriately, Espion or 'spy'.

Once you leave Toucy it is worth making east via minor roads to the fortified village of Diges and then from Riot to Chevannes.

Apart from a church in poor condition and much altered in the nineteenth century, there is little of architectural interest here, but on the northern edge, overlooking a beautifully restored fortified château (now a farm) is La Charmaille, one of the 500 best restaurants in France. In a modernized nineteenth-century farmhouse, the dining room looks out over lawns and a mill-stream, and here you can sample dishes from an interesting menu which are neither expensive nor unduly exotic, and are beautifully prepared and served. Try, for example, the *feuilleté de perche*, their *filet de morue* or duck served on a bed of fresh, lightly cooked young cabbage. The cheese is interesting. Normally you are offered two portions of the same local cow's milk cheese, one older and slightly harder than the other. The wine list is equally restrained but good. Local white wines are much in evidence with inevitably a number of Chablis, but the red from nearby Coulanges-la-Vineuse, made solely from Pinot Noir grapes, is a bargain. Thus fortified you arrive at Auxerre.

Auxerre

Evidence of man's presence on the banks of the Yonne, here as elsewhere, dates from the earliest times. The Gauls developed a small but important centre (Autricum) which was further expanded by the Romans. By the end of the fourth century, Autissiodurum was both administratively and commercially a strategic town on the Via Agrippa north from Arles and leading to Boulogne on the coast. According to local history a bishopric was established here from the late third century, the most celebrated incumbent being undoubtedly Germanus or Saint Germain, after whom the abbey church is named. He was born, probably in Auxerre, in 378 and played a significant part in the spreading of Christianity throughout Roman Gaul. He died in 448 in Ravenna in Italy, and according to his last wishes his body was brought back to Auxerre and buried in a chamber still to be seen beneath the present church. Fifty years later the Benedictine monastery of Saint-Germain was founded by Queen Clotilde, the wife of the Frankish King Clovis, and thereafter Auxerre became a place of pilgrimage whose influence grew over the following 300 years during which time as many as seven churches existed within the town walls. Despite extensive damage by the

Saracens in the eighth century and by the Normans a hundred years later, the monastery remarkably and fortunately remained intact.

Throughout the Middle Ages Auxerre grew in importance. New fortifications were built whose line followed that of the modern *boulevards* which replaced them (as at Sens, for example) in the nineteenth century. During this period the most significant visitor to the town was Joan of Arc. In 1429 she passed through on her way to Chinon with a handful of followers; a few months later she returned triumphant on her way to crown Charles VII at Rheims, this time, so it is reported, with an army of 20,000.

Modern-day Auxerre (pronounced Ausserre) gives the impression of being a lively, bustling provincial town. With a population approaching 50,000 it is nearly twice the size it was immediately after the war, but some local people feel that it has reached a point of stagnation, a result, they say, of narrow-mindedness on the part of the town's administration, and they argue that more industry should be brought to the region, that a university should be created and the train service to Paris and to the south improved. Others, however, are (self) satisfied, enjoy a kind of independence and consider Auxerre to be superior to its rival Sens and entirely worthy of being the *département*'s capital. A stroll around the town certainly gives an impression of considerable wealth, but in addition to welcome government support for the restoration of quite a few buildings the sources of it are changing. The wine trade remains one of them, of course. Even though many of the local vineyards have been swallowed up during the last thirty years or so by urban development, Auxerre is the centre for a number of world-famous and lucrative wines, notably Chablis. There is also a strong boating tradition. Saint Nicholas, patron saint of sailors, looks over the Yonne from his square, and while he may have seen a diminution in commercial transport as road and rail systems have developed and bypassed Auxerre, there has been a welcome expansion in leisure traffic during the last fifteen years in particular.

Anyone visiting Auxerre for the first time should first appreciate it from the Pont Paul-Bert, ideally on a summer evening when the shades of pink and red in the medieval tiles show themselves at their best and subtlest. On a fine, still day the cathedral churches of Saint-Étienne and Saint-Germain, rising above the roofs, are reflected in the Yonne. (It is difficult to imagine the same stretch of water harbouring German submarines during the early 1940s.) From the bridge the path along the right bank takes you to the *port de plaisance* and to a steep pedestrian bridge that crosses the river to the Quai de la République. Just a hundred metres to the right behind a high wall and a forbidding door by the Rue Lebeuf is the terraced garden of the town's *préfecture* (in the former bishop's palace), full of willows and flowering cherries. You catch a glimpse of beautifully restored Romanesque arcading but to get in and inspect it more closely is officially impossible. However, it is worth asking at the main reception in the Rue Cochois or, if this fails, trying to persuade the policeman on duty to allow you to speak to the *huissier*. If you succeed in getting in you will be able to appreciate the splendour of the main hall – a vast room with beautiful beams, tapestries and a view across the river – and admire the quality of the restoration. On the floor below is the vaulted *cellier*, now largely used for official receptions, and along a corridor the Prefect's office, already glimpsed from outside. Here you can examine the twelfth-century arcading which runs the length of the east-facing window and admire the conditions in which some civil servants are privileged to work.

Dominating this part of the town is Saint-Étienne. Tradition has it that the first cathedral on this site was begun by the efforts of one Bishop Amator around 400 and that it grew over the next 500 years before being ravaged by a series of fires in the eleventh century. Hugues de Chalon had the church rebuilt but it was destroyed and completely redesigned a hundred years later by Guillaume de Seignelay, who considered the Romanesque style out of fashion with the new Gothic cathedrals in the Île de France and, of course, at Sens. Of Hugues' church only the crypt remains. Between 1215 and 1525 Saint-Étienne grew to what it is today, a light, elegant, almost fragile building nearly 100 metres long and 34 metres high but only 13 wide. Three features in particular should be noted. First is the thirteenth-century stained glass around the east end with its deep reds and blues, as rich as those at Chartres or Bourges, depicting scenes from the Bible and the lives of various saints. The second is the carvings in the ambulatory; some are sober and dignified, no doubt of local worthies or men of the church, but others are almost surrealistically wild, of beasts, demons, serpents and pagan heads. And the third is the beautiful modern, wooden statue of Saint Germain in the second chapel on the south side of the nave.

With its distinct upward thrust the sense of spirituality in Saint-Étienne is strong, especially when you stand at the crossing, but Hugues' crypt has to be visited not simply for the contrast in style but for the solidity of the faith it symbolizes. Some claim it to be the finest of its kind in Burgundy and it certainly bears comparison with the crypt below Saint-Germain. It is like a miniature church, its massive pillars seemingly squashed by the weight of the choir above. It was once decorated with paintings, of which two remain: one, dating from around 1100, of Christ of the Apocalypse riding a white horse with four angels in adoration, and the other a late thirteenth-century depiction of Christ in Majesty. The treasures, too, deserve to be seen. Mostly these consist of illuminated manuscripts (missals, books of hours, bibles and so on) but there are some delicate Flemish miniatures and the threadbare tunic worn by Saint Germain.

The outside of Saint-Étienne, damaged by the Calvinists who occupied Auxerre in 1567 and again by the Revolutionaries, and badly eroded by the weather (and pigeons) is disappointing and in need of cleaning and restoration. No doubt this will happen and for a superb illustration of what can be achieved when money is made available and the spirit is willing you only have to visit Saint-Germain, where, since the late 1980s, a programme of work due to continue until the end of the century has been under way. Already the chapter house, walled up in the eighteenth century and only rediscovered in the 1970s, has been restored. Its fine Romanesque arches, decorated simply with motifs of lilies or grapes, have led experts to believe that it was probably the inspiration for the chapter house in Vézelay. But what commands attention is the Carolingian crypt which centres around the resting place Saint Germain had prepared for himself. Here you have the distinct feeling of going back deep into history, especially when you learn that some of the oak beams and the lintel bearing the mass of the vaulting are nearly 2000 years old! The crypt also contains the oldest frescoes anywhere in France.

Painted in 858, three semi-circular ones depict the martyrdom of Saint Stephen (Saint Étienne) of which the last has the disembodied hand of God stretching out to receive the saint's soul into heaven as he perishes beneath the stones. An interesting architectural feature of the crypt is a thirteenth-century extension in the form of a rotunda with a vaulted ceiling divided into ten sections. Immediately above is an identical chapel and this double construction is virtually unique in France. In the main vaulting of the crypt itself are four oculi, claimed to have been put there for the purposes of ventilation; it seems probable, however, that they may have been opened up so that the faithful could peer down into this holy place from the church above.

There are plans to bring together on the site of the original abbey the riches of Auxerre's various museums. Already in the dormitory there is a collection of Gallo-Roman material including some extraordinary primitive funerary slabs. It is intended to house a collection of even earlier remains in the room above, and from the stairway joining the two is a splendid view into the church above the choir.

Apart from the Protestant Saint-Pèlerin which stands on the site of the first ever church in Auxerre, two other major ones should be seen. Saint-Pierre-en-Vallée in the Rue Joubert is an ornate classical building which after the Revolution was divided up into apartments. To the west and in its own square is Saint-Eusèbe, whose origins date from 630. As we see it today the church is a mixture of different styles and the tower in particular, despite being in need of attention, is particularly striking. Inside, the sixteenth-century stained glass is in good condition and in a cupboard in the fourth chapel on the south side is a piece of Saint Germain's shroud, in silk with a design in pale blue and gold of eagles and roses.

The eastern half of the town slopes down quite sharply to the river. This is where medieval Auxerre developed with *quartiers* specializing in wine, shipping, leather goods, zinc working and so on, and whose memory lives on, as in Tournus, for example, in street-names. On the whole restoration has been successful and many of the houses from the fifteenth and sixteenth centuries with their attractive roofs and timbering are historic monuments. Interesting and unusual features are numerous. In the Place

Coche d'Eau one house used for occasional exhibitions has large parts of its basement hollowed out of the rock only metres away from the crypt of Saint-Germain. If you go into the house next door and cross the tiny courtyard you will discover an oak spiral staircase which has been there for nearly 500 years.

There are so many of these houses that to indicate individual ones serves little purpose, but a moment should be found to visit the one in the Place des Cordeliers, above a butcher's shop, where the eighteenth-century novelist Restif de la Bretonne served as an apprentice printer. (In the early 1990s a debate was raging about its future. Local conservationists argued that the town should buy it and convert it into a museum but the mayor was refusing to release funds.) Interesting too is the early eighteenth-century Maison de l'Arquebuse, on the edge of the new market place to the south of the town. The annual winner of a bird-shooting competition held since the Middle Ages in the original grounds was exempt from paying taxes for a whole year; anyone who was fortunate enough to win three years in succession had exemption for life!

Back in the pedestrianized centre of Auxerre, two other features should not be neglected: the Passage Manifacier and the Tour de l'Horloge. The former is the town's only covered passage and is, with the Passage de la Halle in Autun, one of the only two in Burgundy. Conceived by a specialist in the arts of glazing, silvering and varnishing, it was opened in 1868 with much publicity in the local press. Restored in recent years after a period of near total neglect it is now a chic arcade with expensive clothes and china shops. Its particular feature is that it joins two streets (the Rue de la Fécauderie and the Rue des Boucheries) on different levels. The entrance in the first is an elegant example of Second Empire design; the second, several metres lower, is reached by a stairway leading down through a rather gloomy Dostoyevskian tenement to a street which in fact marks the limit of the Gallo-Roman centre of Auxerre. Less than 100 metres away, just about in the very centre of the town, is the fifteenth-century clock tower, well restored in 1983. Built on the foundations of one of the Gallo-Roman gates and originally known as the Tour Gaillarde, it is famous for its clock which gives time based on the movements of both sun and moon. The needle indicating the former moves round the clock face in twenty-four hours; the latter loses three quarters of an hour each day. With each new moon, however, the two needles overlap at midday and with each full moon they do so at midnight. In the nineteenth century the tower was topped by a wooden belfry which was manned by local *vignerons* on the lookout for approaching bad weather.

In the mid eighteenth century those responsible for this vigil would have had nearly 2000 hectares in and around Auxerre to be concerned about. Gradually, with the phylloxera crisis in the late nineteenth century but more significantly with urban and commercial development over the last hundred years, this area has almost completely disappeared and only 3 hectares belonging to the psychiatric hospital remain. What you see today are the slopes around Chablis 20 kilometres away, where what is arguably the world's most famous and controversial white wine is produced.

Evidence has been traced for wine having been produced from vines grown in the narrow valley of the Serein as long ago as the seventh century, but systematic exploitation of the hillsides only began in earnest and on a large scale 500 years later when the monks from Pontigny decided that their local supply was inadequate. As Chablis wine became known so demand increased. Throughout the Middle Ages it was exported, mainly to Rouen in Normandy and Paris, whose development during the eighteenth and nineteenth centuries resulted in an even bigger market. But this was when problems began. True Chablis wine is made from the Chardonnay grape alone (known here as the Beaunois) whose yield is relatively small, and in order to satisfy swelling numbers of customers, *vignerons* planted less demanding and more prolific varieties such as Gamay and Sacy. Difficulties of a different kind appeared in the forms of the phylloxera crisis in the late nineteenth century, and of competition as the improved transport system allowed the importation of cheaper wines from the south to the Paris market. And more recently still, competition from the New World wines designated simply as Chablis or Chablis-style has not helped. There is no doubt that *true* Chablis is very distinctive. The Chardonnay is not vinified here as it is further south where the use of oak barrels results in the buttery flavour of white Burgundy;

Chablis' bright, fresh qualities derive instead from the flinty soil and the aspect of the vineyard. But the difficulty of finding it and at an affordable price is considerable. (My own supplier, whose wine has proved consistently good, was recommended to me long ago by a hotel owner in Tonnerre.) Despite the relative uniformity of the soil in the region not all of the vineyards are suitably placed and the mixing of varieties continues. And while there are now quite a number of *vignerons* who do conform to all the required standards they have to contend with a frequently difficult climate. The Serein valley is quite narrow and in periods of frost traps pockets of intensely cold air which can be disastrous in the spring when the flowers are forming. Various methods are employed to combat this, including one – now going out of favour – by which the vines are sprinkled with water which then freezes to form a protective covering of ice! More traditionally, the *vignerons* light fires or bring heaters to their vineyards, and one of the strangest sights in this part of Burgundy is that of the hillsides with their trellises of severely pruned vines, dark against a covering of snow or heavy ground frost and with dozens of coils of smoke rising against a pale blue sky. And a reminder too that the vine-worker's lot is frequently a hard one (even if the owner's profits are substantial) are the *cabanes*, igloo-shaped shelters made from the larger of the stones which are brought down from the higher reaches of the slopes in spring to repair damage caused by erosion during winter. In order to prevent draughts, earth from a trench dug round the hut is piled up against the sides. Fires are lit inside, the only 'chimney' being a hole in the roof. This also allows sunlight in and in times of rain is simply blocked up. Little wonder that young people prefer to try to find work in neighbouring towns or in Paris.

Whatever may be in the bottle, the magic of the Chablis label continues to work, however. During the fourth weekend of November, after the work of the harvest is over, a *fête des vins* is held with a mammoth lunch, dancing and singing. On the Monday the *vignerons* themselves and their personal friends have their own *fête* known as La Pélée to which each person is supposed to contribute two bottles of wine; there is usually every reason to celebrate sales concluded during the previous forty-eight hours. Rather more interesting is a tradition whereby in February one of the villages with the Chablis *appellation* holds a religious service in honour of Saint Vincent and a procession follows the Serein through the vineyards. Chablis itself, badly damaged by a German air-raid in June 1940, has little of architectural interest but is a pleasant enough town in which to spend an hour or so. The church dedicated to Saint Martin, the patron saint of travellers, has been much restored though it does bear traces of its twelfth-century origins. On the door to the south porch a number of horse shoes have been nailed and a local legend holds that one was put there by Joan of Arc on her way to Chinon. Even if you are not able to be here for the '*Saint-Vincent tournante*' in February, the way north to Pontigny through the major villages makes a pleasant excursion at most times of the year and for anyone visiting northern Burgundy the Cistercian abbey church here should not be missed.

The modest west door facing you at the end of an avenue between lime trees gives no idea of the splendour and sense of space inside the church, especially along the side aisles. These, with their clusters of pillars and beautifully symmetrical vaulting, culminating in the nine-bayed roof of the semi-circular apse and the eleven chapels which radiate from it, create the balance and harmony so fundamental to any true Cistercian building. Unlike at Fontenay, clerestory windows allow in enough light to show off the pale, almost white stone to full advantage and it is impossible not to be moved by the spirituality of the place. It was this quality which in the inter-war years prompted Paul Desjardins, a teacher of philosophy, to create a discussion centre here to which he invited eminent literary and intellectual European figures such as François Mauriac, André Malraux, Thomas Mann and T. S. Eliot. The annual gatherings, known as the 'Décades de Pontigny', became internationally famous and, inspired by a spirit of humanism and pacifism, took place in the rebuilt and modernized remains of the abbey buildings. Since 1968 the site has been used as a centre for the re-education and training of physically handicapped young people.

East from Pontigny and over a rising countryside patched with vineyards, arable land and woods, lies Tonnerre on the Armançon and the Canal de Bourgogne, a bustling little town of around 7000 which serves as an ideal departure point for explorations throughout the north-western corner of Burgundy. Its name has nothing to do with thunder. It derives from the Gaulish *durum*, meaning a fort, and Turnus, the name of a mythical god and protector of the first inhabitants, who established themselves on a steep hill overlooking the river and now topped by the church of Saint-Pierre which is currently being restored. Gradually, as the need for this essentially defensive position grew less acute so the town developed on the banks of the river. But even then it was not without its problems. Plaques in a chapel on the north side of the church of Notre-Dame record how in 1632 and 1633 over 3000 people died from a plague. Just under thirty years later in 1660 the entire town was severely damaged by fire. Fortunately Tonnerre's two major features were spared – the area around the Fosse Dionne and the Ancien Hôpital.

At the foot of the same escarpment on which Saint-Pierre stands, the Fosse Dionne or sacred spring (*fons divina*) is one of the most impressive in all Burgundy. It has been estimated that it draws on the water table south of Tonnerre spreading over an area of 50 square kilometres and on average produces 200 litres of water per second, and at times of heavy rain very much more. It has never been properly explored. Attempts in the past have seen divers go nearly 400 metres upstream and to a depth of 61 metres, but the force of the current and the poor visibility have so far proved too daunting. Rather less prosaically, a local tradition claims the spring to be inhabited by a serpent whose look alone is enough to strike anyone dead. The water fills a finely preserved eighteenth-century *lavoir* and then is taken under the main street to a drainage channel (the Bief de Moulins) which eventually runs into the Armançon. A hundred years ago it was used to provide energy for mills and tanneries, of which a few near-derelict examples remain.

The Ancien Hôpital was founded in 1293 by Marguerite de Bourgogne, the young widow of Charles d'Anjou, brother of Saint Louis. Having seen violence and bloodshed during her husband's military escapades in the Holy Lands and in Sicily, she vowed on her return to Tonnerre to do something to care for the sick and needy. The result was a hospital for about forty people which anticipated its far more celebrated equivalent at Beaune by 150 years. As at the Hôtel-Dieu at Beaune, it is arguable that care was directed more at the patients' spiritual well-being than at their physical state and according to local records a resident doctor was not appointed until the 1560s. But even if for most this was where they spent their last days on earth it must have been an airy pleasant place, probably a far cry from their usual living conditions, and the presence of the young queen amongst them would have seemed a blessing in itself. Stripped bare, today the hall is imposing. Nearly 100 metres long with walls 9 metres high rising to a huge roof of oak beams (hidden from the grounds by a false ceiling of chestnut slats), it commands respect, though it has not always done so. After the Revolution and until 1812 it was turned into a grain store, with traders setting up their own shops, and early in the twentieth century a plan to turn it into a permanent covered market was only just reversed by public outcry. One curious feature, which has nothing to do with illness, is the gnomon, a device (like a flat sundial) for measuring the passage of time and its division into months and seasons, carved into the floor. The passage of a point of light admitted through a tiny hole in a blind window is traced on a series of lines and calculations are made accordingly. It was constructed in 1785 by a monk, and traces of the damage caused by cartwheels and horses' hooves during the years of the Revolution can still be seen.

As I have suggested, Tonnerre is ideally placed for anyone wishing to explore further east to Châtillon-sur-Seine and the limits of the Côte d'Or or south-east to Fontenay and Semur-en-Auxois. This wedge of land, divided in the main between Tonnerrois and the Châtillonnais beyond, is as unexplored and as unfamiliar to many who go to Burgundy as the Gâtinais or parts of the Nièvre to the west. From Tonnerre the land rises and falls in large sweeps, given over largely to grain but with clumps of woodland, and cut by narrow valleys where villages and clusters of houses have formed in search of water. The basic rock here is limestone, and quarries and cement works, even if they are unsightly, provide a source of income for many. In the Châtillonnais, on average nearly 100 metres higher, there are more areas of forest, iron ore as well as limestone, and it is clear that, as around Montceau-les-mines south of the Morvan, considerable industrial activity has flourished since the thirteenth century. Today agriculture dominates the commercial life of the region but many of the forges, now replaced by modern factories, remain, and just as elsewhere anyone so disposed can follow a *route des vins*, in the Châtillonnais there is a rather less seductive *itinéraire sidérurgique* ('iron- and steelmaking route') between Châtillon and Montbard. Châtillon-sur-Seine, which came to prominence in the ninth century when the bishop of Langres had the relics of Saint Vorles transferred there, was for long a frontier town. Indeed, until the seventeenth century the right bank of the Seine belonged to Langres, the left to the dukes of Burgundy. More recently the town enjoyed a strategic importance. Joffre set up his headquarters there at the beginning of World War I and as France was liberated in 1944 the triumphant armies of De Lattre and Leclerc joined forces only a few kilometres outside the town at Nod-sur-Seine.

Having been badly damaged by German air raids in 1940 most of Châtillon's old centre has disappeared. Fortunately the church dedicated to Saint Vorles was spared. Of tenth-century origin, this was where the Virgin Mary appeared to Bernard and offered him milk from her breast, and set him on his lifetime's spiritual crusade. On a small hill to the south-east of the town, it is backed by an impressive cemetery and parkland with lime trees and poplars, from which there are views of the Seine curling north across expanses of rich arable land and south towards the Forêt de Chamesson and beyond to its source about 50 kilometres away. A hundred metres or so beyond the cemetery wall (originally part of a château belonging to the dukes of Burgundy) and at the foot of a cliff face is the Source de la Douix which, bigger than the Dionne at Tonnerre, produces several hundred litres of water per second. This extra water flowing into the Seine ensured that for many months of the year small boats could begin the long and hazardous journey towards Paris and north-western France, ensuring important trading links from early times. Evidence for such activity has been uncovered since the 1930s at Vix, 7 kilometres north of Châtillon, where a community of some importance dating from around 600 BC is known to have existed. However what was common knowledge was suddenly given international fame in 1953 by a local farmer's discovery of an Iron Age burial chamber which contained a funeral bier bearing the skeleton of a woman elaborately adorned with jewels and gold.

Inside the tomb as well was a huge bronze vase, almost 2 metres high, beautifully worked with a frieze depicting chariots each drawn by four horses and foot-soldiers carrying massive round shields. Each handle of the bowl (large enough to carry 1100 litres of liquid) is supported by the bust of a gorgon whose body is entwined erotically by snakes. The Vase de Vix, thought to have been made by a Greek craftsman in southern Italy, together with the other jewels and artefacts from the tomb, are on display in Châtillon's museum, the Maison Philandrier. It alone makes a visit to the town imperative.

Between the N71, which follows the valley of the Seine, and the departmental border about 30 kilometres away the landscape to the south is dominated by forests, especially by the 10,000 hectares of the Forêt de Châtillon, almost to the outskirts of Dijon. Minor roads and tracks enable you to penetrate the very heart of this region and sample the delights of its tiny villages: Rochefort, with its modern château and disused forges reflected in the waters of a pretty *étang* bordered with thick clumps of reeds; Essarois, where there are the remains of a temple dedicated to Apollo; Barjon, with the eighth-century tomb of a hermit known as Saint-Frou which used to attract those in lingering ill-health in search of a miraculous cure; or Moloy, with its fourteenth-century frescoes of the Virgin and of saints Anne, Michael and Laurence. Less agreeable and uncomfortably near by is one of France's deeply hidden nuclear research centres. Slightly to the north, on the very border with the *département* of Haute-Marne, a number of other villages bear witness to the presence of the Knights Templar in the form of their rather severe architecture: Voulaines-les-Templiers has a fifteenth-century tower remaining from the original fort; the remains of another are to be seen on a large farmstead in an area called Épailly; and at Bure-les-Templiers excavations have enabled archaeologists to reconstruct the plan of the Knights' property. In most cases the scale not only underlines the power and prestige of these white-cloaked Christian warriors, but suggests that they enjoyed a life-style which went some way beyond the simplicity to which they were supposedly committed.

If instead of exploring this distant corner of northern Burgundy you leave Tonnerre for Semur, then follow the Armançon and

Canal de Bourgogne. Within 10 kilometres is Tanlay. Here you find a château, built on the site of an older one in the sixteenth and seventeenth centuries, which most commentators consider the 'most celebrated' or 'beautiful' or simply 'best' in Burgundy. I have to confess that I find it pompous, too grand and simply out of place. But be that as it may there is no doubt that it deserves attention. The oldest part is an elaborate gate house called the Petit Château, the work of François d'Andelot, in the style of a triumphal arch. Beyond this is the entrance proper flanked by two obelisks, the work of d'Andelot's successor, Pierre Le Muet, who completed the main building and designed the water system and moat. The château is built around a courtyard with round, squat towers in the front corners capped by hemispherical domes of slates which in turn are topped with lanterns. These wings join with the central block, which has two front towers containing staircases and at the rear two more round ones, on three floors, overlooking the grounds. The whole roof is elaborately decorated and has numerous outshot windows. Privately owned – it has belonged to the same family for nearly 350 years – the château is open to the public. The monumental fireplaces for which Le Muet seems to have been responsible are of particular note, as is the rich wood carving in the reception room, the *salon de compagnie*. On the first floor a painted ceiling depicting dignatories of the sixteenth century as mythological figures always draws attention; with Diane de Poitiers as Venus, the Duc de Guise as Mars or the future Henri II as the two-faced Janus, its aim seems gently satirical. The château is a major tourist attraction and as a *monument historique* benefits from government support, but a sign of the economic problems faced by anyone trying to maintain such a place was the preparatory work in the early 1990s for a small golf course within the grounds.

Altogether more agreeable, to my taste, is the château at Ancy-le-Franc, at least from the outside. More severe and restrained than Tanlay, it was probably designed in the mid sixteenth century by an Italian, Sebastiano Serlio, who was brought to France by François I, though some think the work is by one of his admirers, Pierre Lescot. The planning of the grounds was given to Le Nôtre, who also designed those at Versailles. Prints of the château in the late seventeenth century show a majestic building enclosed by a modest moat (filled in 200 years later) and surrounded by symmetrically planned gardens with alleyways, hedges, shrubberies and fountains. Unfortunately none of these remains, but the château has an elegance (if rather seedy) and sense of proportion which are lacking at Tanlay. The inside is richly decorated with wall and ceiling paintings of classical, mythological and historical subjects, many restored, many still in poor condition. Once again the economic problems created by the management of a property of this size are reflected in the present owner's practice of using the château for receptions and business seminars, having a museum of vintage cars in some of the outbuildings and opening the grounds for music festivals.

Just about half-way between Ancy-le-Franc and Semur the road passes the Grande Forge de Buffon which is named after Georges-Louis Leclerc, Comte de Buffon. An eighteenth-century aristocrat and scholar, he was for a while overseer of Louis XV's gardens before withdrawing to Burgundy where he first wrote his celebrated *Histoire naturelle* and then, during the last two decades of his life, experimented with iron smelting. At the height of their productivity his forges employed over 300 people and, if not exactly a cooperative, the whole venture was certainly one in which everyone was fully involved. In 1979 his buildings and machinery were completely restored and opened to the public, as were the offices and workers' lodgings. Of all the forges in this part of Burgundy, Buffon's was certainly the most famous and in fact continued to produce iron until the 1860s.

If a forge of the complexity of this one is a little surprising in the mid eighteenth century, an even earlier example was fully operational a hundred years earlier at the nearby Abbaye de Fontenay, and there is evidence that soon after the abbey's completion around 1200 the monks had begun to exploit the local iron ore. But it is not for this that Fontenay is famous. Founded only five years after Bernard's arrival at Cîteaux, the abbey grew during the Middle Ages to be one of the most influential and important of the Cistercian order, certainly in northern France. The buildings are set classically in Cistercian fashion low in a shallow valley and surrounded by forest, and it is impossible not to sense even today the order's belief in humility and the need to withdraw from life, though to do so you have to go there well out of the tourist season. Having reached its high point with around 300 monks in the late Middle Ages, the abbey gradually declined (eight monks only in 1790), and after the Revolution the buildings, whose fabric was already damaged by water and the damp atmosphere, were sold. During the nineteenth century they housed a papermaking factory before being bought in 1906 by the Aynard family whose members are still responsible for the magnificent restoration and maintenance.

If the abbey's setting is totally at one with Saint Bernard's requirements so too are the buildings. These are severe and austere, devoid of practically all ornamentation and comfort. The church, with no side windows, is like a long dark vault, lit only from the east end; the monks' dormitory on the south side is a beautifully proportioned room with a magnificent chestnut roof, but the absence of glass in the windows is a reminder of the conditions in which the monks slept on their straw mattresses. Only the *chauffoir* (apart from the forge and kitchens) was allowed any heating; this was so that the ink used for the illumination of manuscripts would not freeze! Even the cloister with its double arches seems to underline the need for solid contemplation rather than recreation or relaxation. When I visited Fontenay for the first time I can remember only too well that it was under snow and buffeted by gusts of wind, causing me to reflect that 500 years ago the faith required to stay here must have been very strong!

An equally impressive but different site lies 15 kilometres further south at Alise-Sainte-Reine, which takes its name from Alésia, the Celtic fort on the Mont Auxois which Caesar besieged in 52 BC. Already in the spring of the same year the Romans had been defeated by the Gauls led by Vercingetorix. Encouraged by success, he tried again, only on this occasion to be defeated himself, whereupon he withdrew with an army of 80,000 to Alésia while he tried to summon auxiliary troops. Given the hilly nature of the land Caesar decided to besiege the Gauls: an inner line of ditches and stakes prevented the Gauls from leaving their camp, an outer one was a defence against the relief army. When it eventually did come it was defeated and, despite a brave last attempt by Vercingetorix to break out, the siege and battle were over. The Gaulish leader surrendered and six years later was executed by strangulation in Rome. This battle has traditionally been taken by historians to mark the end of a predominantly Gallic civilization by a Gallo-Roman one and the beginnings of modern France. In 1865 a massive statue of Vercingetorix by Aimé Millet was erected on the Mont Auxois about a kilometre to the west of the site of the encampment. The Gaulish leader with his short tunic and hands resting on his sword looks sternly into the distance; it is said that beneath the mane of hair and large, drooping moustache are the features of Napoleon III, who was responsible for inaugurating the first excavations of the battle ground. Most of what remains of the siege material has been discovered over the years, but reburied to protect it from rain and frost; however, a splendid reproduction of part of Caesar's wall can be inspected at the Archéodrome just south of Beaune. While most of the items dug up from the battlefield are on display in the national museum at Saint-Germain-en-Laye to the west of Paris, the Musée Alésia in the village has a small collection of weapons, including some particularly nasty sharpened stakes (oddly called 'stimuli') which, half-buried in the ground, were designed to make any foot soldier's progress a painful business. The museum also contains relics from the Gallo-Roman town which existed here for the next four centuries, and you can explore the excavated remains with their clear evidence of a temple, public meeting house and shops with the help of a detailed plan provided by the museum.

On leaving Alésia a minor road follows the valley of the Ozerain. After about 2 kilometres Flavigny is signposted to the right, at over 400 metres, a true *village perché* surrounded by forest which, as all the guidebooks remind us, was once compared with Jerusalem by the early nineteenth-century writer Chateaubriand. For many years the village lay neglected, inhabited essentially only by monks from both Dominican and Benedictine communities. Now, while still important religiously, it has become a major feature on the tourist trail across northern Burgundy and has seen many of its houses bought – but restored as a consequence – by Germans and Swiss. Once inside the walls you can wander at will and enjoy the many medieval features of what is becoming almost an open-air museum – gargoyles, statuettes, windows, cellars, doorways, stair-turrets and so on.

If you enter Flavigny by the fifteenth-century Porte du Bourg, whose military appearance is softened by a statue of the Virgin Mary in a niche above the central arch, the road leads directly to the parish church of Saint-Genès. Much restored, it is unremarkable architecturally, but the choir-stalls have (or had) a number of delightful, witty and realistic carvings. One still depicts a woman sitting with a cat on her lap, another a stern teacher reading a lesson to his pupils, another a monk holding his nose with a book open on his knees. Originally there were many more of these carvings but in 1978 the church was vandalized and nearly all were sawn off. As a result Saint-Genès is often locked.

To the west side of the town, just inside the Porte Sainte-Barbe, is the site of the abbey of Saint-Pierre, most of which was pulled down in the early nineteenth century and is now occupied by a factory specializing in aniseed sweets. Fortunately the ninth-century crypt and ambulatory above it have been in large part preserved.

Further west still is the double entrance of the Porte du Val, whose squat round towers are a stern reminder of the need for stout fortifications 600 years ago. Immediately alongside are the grounds and church belonging to the Maison Lacordaire, which takes its name from the reforming Dominican priest Henri Lacordaire (1802–61). Having for a while been a retirement home for women it now houses an important seminary of the right-wing integrist movement within the French Catholic church, whose headquarters are the church of Saint-Nicolas-en-Chardonnet in Paris. Its reputation in the village is mixed.

From Flavigny the road follows an attractive ridge overlooking the local forest and across to Hauteroche and Gissey before crossing the main road from Montbard and the canal. This is the central part of the Auxois, a countryside of rich pastureland spotted with spurs of rock, some, like the one at Flavigny, topped by villages. Finally, no visit to this part of Burgundy would be complete without time spent in Semur-en-Auxois and Époisses.

Semur

From Flavigny, Semur can be reached by crossing the D905 and continuing west along the minor road which links up with the D954. However, a far more dramatic approach is from the west.

Here you rediscover the Armançon, which skirts a great promontory of pink granite from which rise the round towers of the fourteenth-century château; one of them, the Tour de l'Orle d'Or, has an alarming crack running down it. The fact that the tower houses the premises of Semur's Société des Sciences and a small museum suggests that no-one is particularly worried, however. If you cross the river by the Pont Joly you climb up to the Rue du Rempart and follow the line of the fortifications past the grounds of the former hospital to the Pont Pinard which, opposite Joly, marks the centre of Semur today. From here eastwards you enter the Rue Buffon, a cobbled area now in principle pedestrianized and forming the commercial centre of the town, which you leave to the east through the double gates, the Porte Guillier and the Porte Sauvigny. Just before them is the church of Notre-Dame, begun early in the twelfth century. A slim, delicate building with tall west towers and a central spire on an octagonal base, it is an illustration of the complete gamut of Gothic styles but its exterior has suffered from erosion and damage and is badly in need of attention. Fortunately the tympanum above the north door depicting the legend of Saint Thomas taking the gospels to India remains as, rather more frivolously, do two snails carved into a column on the left-hand side. Inside, the light from the high clerestory windows creates a quite different atmosphere from, say, Fontenay. I personally find it fussy but there are some attractive features – the intricate and delicately sculpted fifteenth-century ciborium, the polychrome group depicting the entombment of Christ from the same century or the sixteenth-century statue of Saint Sebastian from which the arrows have been removed leaving his body marked simply by holes. On the north side, two chapels contain stained-glass windows originally given to the church by the drapers' and butchers' guilds in the Middle Ages and depicting their trades. Several are nineteenth-century replacements but the style and colours are uniform. The one of a butcher about to bury his axe in the neck of an understandably anxious-looking bullock is especially lively.

Once you leave Semur both Dijon and Auxerre are within an hour's drive by the nearby motorway and the edge of the Morvan is even closer. But do not miss Époisses. This tiny village of less than 1000 inhabitants is famous for two reasons, its château and its cheese. From Semur a picturesque road cuts across farmland past the Forêt de Saint-Loup and enters the village from the north. The château in its extensive grounds lies to the right on a small tributary of the Serein and, apart from some modifications in the sixteenth and nineteenth centuries in particular, has been here in its present form for about 600 years. From the road you pass through the first of two lines of fortifications into an area containing a row of houses, a small church, outbuildings, the village school and a dovecote containing 3000 nesting boxes. When you realize that each one of these corresponded to one and a half hectares of land you have some idea of the size of the original estate. As at Ratilly the revolving-ladder mechanism for collecting eggs remains intact. Such an arrangement of buildings suggests not only that the entire village could be protected within the château's outer walls at times of danger or war but also that relations between owners and villagers were generally good. Despite that, half the château was deliberately destroyed after the Revolution and the Guitaut family was imprisoned; when they were released they returned to find a semi ruin and had to embark on an arduous, expensive but ultimately successful programme of reconstruction of the main part. This you can now see beyond the second line of fortifications, fronted by a terraced lawn with an elegant well. Unfortunately the château is not open to the public but records show that it has received numerous visitors of rank and fame including Henri IV, Louis XIII and Chateaubriand, and it is said that Louis XIV was conceived here. Madame de Sévigné, whose grandmother lived at the nearby Château de Bourbilly, was a frequent guest at Époisses and wrote warmly of its beauty and grandeur.

About 200 metres from the château along the main street and to the left is the village cheese cooperative. Here you can buy the local product made from whole cow's milk, washed after three days in lightly salted water and frequently again three or four weeks later in the traditional Burgundian spirit made from grapes and known as *marc*. Traditionally the cheese is sold wrapped in imitation vine leaves and boxed, and normally requires two to three months before it is ready for eating. Variations of this pungent, creamy *Époisses artisanal* can be found throughout the region and the market in Semur usually offers several. Related kinds such as L'Ami du Chambertin or Le Langres can also be found further afield. At present Époisses is not subject to strict controls — the kind of spirit used for washing or the necessary maturing time (*affinage*) — and, as in the case of Chablis wine, some that is not entirely as it should be does find its way on to shelves. Gradually, however, things are improving and the real Époisses is both unmistakable and an experience not to be missed. Perhaps this is why the château here is one of my favourites in all Burgundy.

2
Dijon

When Lawrence Durrell's friend the notorious American novelist Henry Miller arrived in Dijon as a young man to take up a post as a teacher of English, his first impressions seem not to have been very favourable. Years later in *Tropic of Cancer* he wrote: 'Silent, empty gloom – that's how it impressed me. A hopeless, jerk-water town where mustard is turned out in carload lots, in vats and tuns and barrels and pots and cute-looking little jars.' Whether many would have shared this opinion more than half a century ago is open to debate (and Miller did revise his view), but it is likely that even his initial reaction today would have been different. It is true of course that any number of provincial capitals in France come to mind as being bigger, more influential and wealthier than Dijon: Aix, spoiled by its Mediterranean microclimate and with its imitation Parisian chic; Bordeaux, smug in its (rival) reputation as one of the great wine meccas of the world; Orléans, with its high technology and sense of historical importance; or Strasbourg, one of the great frontier towns and central to the new Europe. Despite its quarter of a million people Dijon belongs to a different league, alongside the likes of Angers, Chartres, Rheims or Limoges, for example. Different, but in no way qualitatively inferior. At the end of the twentieth century Dijon proudly and quite properly makes much of the quality of life enjoyed by its inhabitants (*dijonnais*), of the fact that it is

France's most ecologically aware town – a fitting tribute to the efforts of its mayor Robert Poujade, who was France's first minister for the environment. Everywhere the slogan *'Dijon ville verte'* catches the eye, and even in a brief visit the high proportion of beautifully tended parks and gardens quickly becomes evident. The members of the present town council have every right to be proud of their achievements and Dijon is one of those towns which deserve to be visited by anyone interested in the true character of provincial France.

In the late twentieth century Dijon can be reached easily by road and rail, such links with other places in and outside France reflecting its growing importance as Europe assumes new dimensions and significance. From Paris the A38 splits away from the A6 at the junction of Pouilly-en-Auxois, ensuring fast access by car. High-speed trains complete the same journey in just over 90 minutes. Lyon, Geneva and Luxembourg are already within easy reach as, by the end of the century, will be Brussels and the Channel Tunnel. While at present air traffic is less developed than road or rail, the terminal at Longvic to the south-east, still used predominantly for military purposes, is seeing an increase in the number of commercial flights linking Dijon with Paris and other towns. Only connections by water seem unlikely to flourish. The Canal de Bourgogne, finished with much optimism in 1833, is now more than anything a tourist attraction and whatever the ecological advantages, the idea of linking the Rhône with the Rhine to form a vast network of commercially exploitable waterways seems to have little future. Had Dijon benefited from a major river the case might have been different, but the Ouche, which rises just outside the village of Lusigny about 50 kilometres to the south-west, curves north to pass south of the town centre and eventually continues in a great loop back to join the Saône 35 kilometres to the south-east at Saint-Jean-de-Losne, is of little consequence. (In 1964 Félix Kir, Dijon's celebrated mayor between 1945 and 1968, quite sensibly had it dammed in order to create a lake (Le Lac Kir) thereby providing his town with a much-needed expanse of water which is immensely popular and extensively used for recreational purposes.) But this apart, the people of Dijon see no need to worry. They envisage their future as part not just of France but of Europe. They believe they have a role to play as a meeting place on the principal trade and tourist routes criss-crossing the continent and at present at least seem little interested in trying to change Dijon's character and strengths. There will, undoubtedly, be an increase in population. Quetigny to the east, whose population has already increased more than twenty-fold since the mid 1950s and which is already part of the greater conurbation, will surely expand further and there must be a danger that the rich, alluvial lands will gradually be invaded by high-density dwellings. Fortunately, since the early 1960s, when Dijon's initial expansion to the west resulted in some insensitive building programmes, care has been taken to ensure that a reasonable balance is maintained between concrete blocks and natural vegetation. It is also unlikely that the commercial and industrial profile of Dijon will alter. The late twentieth-century trend in France towards decentralization will possibly have some effect, but Dijon's present strengths in support industries and as one of the principal gastronomic centres of Europe would seem not to be at risk. And, anticipating the twenty-first century, the university continues to grow in reputation and size reflecting not only a national commitment to high-quality technical, technological and intellectual training but continuing a tradition for learning and culture that Dijon has proudly enjoyed for six centuries.

Most authorities are in agreement that the first substantial reference to Dijon is to be found in the sixth-century *Histoire des Francs* by Gregory of Tours. He describes it as follows:

A fortress with solid walls surrounded by a smiling plain, of rich fertile soil producing crops in abundance. To the south is the river Ouche, full of fish; from the north a stream runs in through one gate, passes beneath a bridge and flows out through another gate. In this way the walls are surrounded by water which drives a number of mills with wonderful efficiency.

There are four doors facing the cardinal points; thirty-three towers reinforce the walls which are made of flint up to a height of twenty feet topped with smaller stones. In all they are thirty feet high and fifteen feet thick.

What precisely the reasons for the development of this fortified encampment were is not clear. Evidence for the earlier existence on this site of ancient religious cults and their followers have been found and it may well be that the Romans built it in this form as protection. The site was certainly on a military route from Lyon to Mainz and therefore worth protecting, but it also seems to have developed as a trading centre. The etymology of the name Dijon is generally held to be Devomagos or Diviomagus, a sacred market, and ancient stone slabs with carvings depicting butchers cutting meat and the selling of groceries, now to be seen in the town's archaeological museum, would seem to bear this out. Quite how accurate Gregory's description was is impossible to say, but from research and the evidence of excavations it appears to be close. Today the line of the walls is clearly indicated and easily followed, and a plaque on the outside of the ducal palace carries a plan. In all it covered about 11 hectares, was nearly 400 metres across at its widest part and had a perimeter of about 1200 metres. The best point at which to have some sense of what the old fortified town was like is just off the Rue Charrue near the Place des Cordeliers, where the tower known as the Tour de Saint Bénigne and converted in the Middle Ages to a chapel is to be found. Possibly Benignus was a missionary priest from Lyon martyred in the second century by being (according to a small statue in the crypt beneath the cathedral bearing his name) impaled on an X-shaped cross. The founding of Christianity in Dijon is certainly attributed to him, his tomb having been 'discovered' subsequently in the early sixth century, and today his resting place in the mortuary chapel beneath the rotunda at the east end of the cathedral is a place of pilgrimage on 1 November.

When in the mid fifth century Langres to the north-east was attacked and sacked by Germanic tribes the bishop (probably Urbain) fled to Dijon for protection. His successors established themselves and remained another 500 years, during which time they were responsible for the creation of the Christian centre of the town just to the west of the Roman camp, with the cathedral church dedicated to Saint Étienne, a chapel to the Virgin Mary and a baptistry under the protection of Saint Vincent, the patron saint of wine makers. Subject to all kinds of disputes during the early Middle Ages, but fortunately spared the violent attentions of the Arabs in the eighth century, when Autun was captured and many monasteries ransacked, Dijon was eventually taken by the king of France, Robert le Pieux, in 1015 and seventeen years later granted the status of a capital. For a century the town grew rapidly and most of the present inner suburbs out as far as the ringroad came into existence. Then in 1137 tragedy struck. The entire town was swept by fire which caused widespread damage and killed many. But under the energetic leadership of the duke, Hugues II, reconstruction began. New outer walls were built with twelve gates, all of which had been pulled down or fallen into decay by the late nineteenth century. The monumental arch known as the Porte Guillaume marks the site of one. Beyond the walls areas of land yet to be developed were marked out and gradually whole new *quartiers* developed, embracing vineyards and small farm plots. Inside the walls weavers, barrel-makers, leather-workers, cobblers, glove-makers, potters all flourished, their trades still recalled in the names of many streets. A coinage was struck and as a result Dijon began to attract moneylenders. A new era was being born.

From the late twelfth century and for the next 150 years Dijon developed steadily as a free city. The scene was set in Burgundy for the accession to power in 1364 of the dukes of the Valois dynasty – Philippe le Hardi (1342–1404), Jean sans Peur (1404–19), Philippe le Bon (1419–67) and Charles le Téméraire (1467–77) – who would rule with skill and much magnificence for over a century. The dukes were different in character. Philippe le Hardi is reputed to have lived life to the full. Portraits frequently show him to be sumptuously dressed; he loved banquets and tournaments. He had a keen sense for administering his town and when in 1369, aged 37, he married Marguerite de Flandres, the richest heiress in Europe, he became the most powerful prince in the whole of Christendom. In order to ensure that he and his heirs would not be forgotten he had a mausoleum built at the Chartreuse de Champmol. His own tomb, designed by Jean de Merveille and Claus Sluter, was richly decorated with marble and alabaster, and may be seen today in the Musée des Beaux Arts. But his taste for grandeur proved to be a severe drain on his wealth and when he died (in Flanders) his sons were obliged to pawn the family's jewels and silver in order to raise enough money to pay for their father's body to be brought back in state (a journey in those days of three months) as well as for the sumptuous funeral ceremony. Philippe's successor, Jean, was ambitious and a bitter rival of Louis d'Orléans, the brother of the king of France, Charles VI. Legend has it that Louis' emblem was a gnarled stick and that Jean deliberately adopted as his a carpenter's plane to indicate that he would eventually get the better of him. He was true to his word: in 1407 he had him murdered. Conflict with the French culminating in the famous battle between the Armagnacs and Burgundians in 1418 seriously drained French military strength to the distinct advantage of the predatory English. Aware of this, Jean sought a reconciliation with the future king of France, Charles VII, but at the meeting held on 11 September 1419 at Montereau he in turn was murdered.

It is interesting that in Shakespeare's *Henry V*, Jean is portrayed as a negotiator and as a man of eloquence; not as a man of war. In his desire for revenge against the French it was hardly surprising that Jean's son Philippe should decide to ally himself with the English, and in 1430 he committed what has been regarded by many as one of the great acts of betrayal in French history: he handed Joan of Arc over to the English for the huge sum of 10,000 gold crowns. Yet Philippe became reconciled with Charles VII four years later and found himself at the head of a nation which stretched from Mâcon in the south to the northern coast of Holland. Under his guidance Burgundy became rich, powerful and awesome. But Philippe also encouraged art and learning and Dijon in particular prospered under his guidance; by the time of his death it had also doubled in size to over 10,000 inhabitants. In addition to his general predilection for fine living, Philippe created in 1429 the order of the Toison d'Or, a kind of company of Christian knights ('*vingt trois chevaliers gentilz hommes de nom et d'armes et sans reproche, nés et procrées en légal mariage*') which, like the English Order of the Garter, survives until today.

Of the four Valois dukes the last, Charles, is, politically at least, perhaps the most famous, though he probably spent less time in Dijon than any of his predecessors. An active, ambitious man, he was determined to turn the dukedom of Burgundy into a kingdom and as part of his schemes he attempted to ensure the support of the English and of Edward IV by marrying the king's sister, Margaret of York. As the chronicler Commines once remarked of him: '*Il désirait grande gloire.*' But as his name indicates

Charles was indeed 'rash'. He lost the support of Edward, continued in his attempts to increase the size of Burgundy by annexing more territories beyond its borders and ran into fierce opposition from René de Lorraine. Ever ambitious, he laid siege to Nancy in January 1477 but the Lorraine defence, with help from the Swiss, was too much for him and he was killed. His body is said to have been found two days later in a frozen swamp half-eaten by wolves.

Whatever their roles in the political evolution of France the activities and interests of the four Valois dukes unquestionably brought status and confidence to both Burgundy and Dijon. After Charles' death, tired of disputes and wary of there being too much power in some of the provinces, Louis XI claimed much of Burgundy for France and appointed a governor who had a castle built for himself, much to the indignation of the local people. This general strengthening of the town continued and was put to the test in 1513 when an army – reputedly 30,000 strong – of Swiss, Germans and Franc-Comtois attacked and laid siege to Dijon for a week early in September. The governor, Louis de Trémouille, who had only six or seven thousand men at his disposal, had no hope of withstanding the onslaught. His first attempt at negotiation having failed, La Trémouille is said to have had the inspired idea of offering wine to the assailants. Its effect was almost instant. Within hours the siege was lifted and a treaty was agreed whereby France would pay 400,000 crowns. The king ultimately refused to pay, on the grounds that the conditions under which it had been drawn up were improper, but Dijon had been saved. A rather more sober account records that the Virgin Mary intervened on the town's behalf and a tapestry on display in the Musée des Beaux Arts shows the good citizens of Dijon parading through the streets bearing her statue from the church of Notre-Dame. In the foreground the soldiers with pikes raised outside the walls appear suitably impressed.

Controlled now directly by the French crown, Dijon could add security to its past glories. During the seventeenth and early eighteenth centuries an important new class developed: an aristocracy based on merit and effort (the *noblesse de robe*) rather than on inheritance (the *noblesse d'épée*). Its influence and prestige can be seen in the city centre in much domestic architecture with magnificent doorways and wrought-iron work (the Hôtel Liégard on Rue Vauban, or the Hôtel Fyot-de-Mimeure by the Palais de Justice) and in a number of monuments. Some particularly striking examples are to be found in the neo-classical Palais des États opposite the Place de la Libération. Other signs of the kind of status which Dijon was increasingly enjoying during the eighteenth century were the foundation of an archbishopric in 1731, with the church of Saint-Étienne becoming the first cathedral and Jean Bouher its incumbent, and the creation in 1723 of the Académie de Dijon, followed in 1750 by the university. We should not forget that all of this was taking place in a town that was still relatively small. By 1800 there were only 21,000 inhabitants; while this figure would multiply threefold during the next century, it was as though Dijon was clinging to its independent, proud past, dealing for preference in quality rather than quantity. Certainly through the years of the wars of religion (from which the town emerged strongly Catholic), the revolution of 1789 and its aftermath, or the social disturbances of the nineteenth century, Dijon stood, if not unscathed, at least not profoundly disturbed. In 1789, for example, some destruction did occur, notably of the Chartreuse de Champmol and the rotunda in Saint-Bénigne, but by and large aristocratic families were spared. Relationships across society appear on the whole to have been good.

The nineteenth century, with the development of the French railway system in particular, brought new prosperity and a population boom. During the first half of the twentieth century numbers increased steadily, but since the 1960s a general fall in the birthrate (which reflects national trends) and a degree of de-urbanization as people move to the countryside have led to some stability. But Dijon is in no danger of losing its rank. While it is unlikely ever to become important industrially, its position as a focal point for European routes is assured. And it will always attract tourists and French alike from far and wide, not just for its architectural treasures, but for the gastronomic delights celebrated every year in early November by the Foire Gastronomique Internationale. Created in 1921 by the then Mayor Gaston Gérard, the Foire attracts thousands.

The Parc des Expositions where it is held, to the north-east of the town centre, is easily reached by twenty minutes' brisk walk or by bus. People are already queuing before opening times at half-past nine or ten in the morning, and the Foire remains busy until closing time, which at weekends is not until half-past eleven at night. Although essentially a commercial venture, this is also a serious celebration of food and drink. The stalls are colourful, often decorated in regional styles. Incongruities – people promoting encyclopedias, skiing holidays or rare books – are soon forgotten as the senses of sight and smell attempt to come to terms with an astonishing array of food and drink. Shellfish, patisserie, meat, patés, bread, cheese, charcuterie, chocolate, snails, oysters and preserved fruit constitute a gastronomic orgy of considerable proportion – and temptation. And there is the drink as well. Beer may make a token appearance as does whisky but inevitably the grape dominates – cognac, armagnac, *marc de bourgogne* and wine. While pride of place is given to local wines there are others from all over France: delicious *vin jaune* from the Jura to the east of Burgundy will be found alongside a selection from Pomerol or Saint Emilion from south-west France; crisp Alsatian wine will be on offer beside luscious dessert wines from Sauternes, Barsac or Monbazillac; delicate rosés from Provence, Champagne or inky Châteauneuf du Pape will attempt to rival the more local wines; dry, flinty Chablis at times almost pale green in colour; heavy, pungent reds from Vosne-Romanée or Pommard; lighter instantly quaffable ones from Givry or Rully; rich, buttery whites from Meursault or the Montrachets. Sampling is easy and local people are soon observed and heard discussing relative merits.

For commercial visitors and serious buyers there is a series of meals constructed around one of the great Burgundian wines, often from a single *domaine*, from villages such as Meursault, Puligny-Montrachet or Aloxe-Corton for example. These take place in rooms just off the main hall which are temporarily transformed into dining-rooms of some splendour, with tables covered with immaculately laundered table-cloths and a magnificent array of cutlery and wine glasses. Serious imbibing and equally serious negotiating take place in these rooms as vintages are discussed, tasted and bought.

For most people such gastronomic heights are beyond consideration. More modestly, it is possible to lunch or dine in the fair on a plate of choucroûte and Alsatian sausage, a *croque monsieur* or even a pizza with a generous glass or two of wine, a *flûte de champagne* or a tawny coloured *armagnac hors d'âge*. By the late evening the noise level has risen considerably. Whole families, especially at the weekend, who have come for their annual outing, fill the temporary restaurants. For them the event is almost like one on the religious calendar, such is the gravity with which food and drink are considered in this part of France.

There are, as we have already noted, a number of characteristic Burgundian dishes, but no account of Dijon's role as the region's capital would be complete without reference to its *pain d'épice*, its mustard (whatever Henry Miller may have thought) and its *cassis*.

Pain d'épice, more a cake than a bread, has a long history, with references to its having been eaten by people as different as the ancient Romans and the Chinese. Traditionally made from rye flour, honey and spices, it was believed to have medicinal properties. The best *pain d'épice* in medieval France was supposed to come from Rheims, but by the early eighteenth century there are references to its being sold in Dijon, and a hundred years later to the first manufacturer, one Barnabé Boittier. Nowadays it is made from wheat flour instead of rye, and again tradition has it that this in fact reflects the preference of Marguerite, Philippe le Hardi's wife.

Of even longer standing is mustard, with references to its manufacture found as long ago as the fourth century. By the Middle Ages it was certainly much in demand, and popular history claims that when Philippe de Valois was entertained in Dijon in 1336 three hundred quarts of it were consumed. Like *pain d'épice*, mustard was for centuries thought to have medicinal properties as well. According to one authority, quoted by the nineteenth-century writer Alexandre Dumas, it could cure scurvy and apoplexy, paralysis and toothache:

> *Possédant le don merveilleux*
> *De chasser le scorbut et la paralysie*
> *De ses esprits vitaux stimulant l'énergie.*
> *Quiconque en savourait pouvait sans accident*
> *Narguer l'apoplexie et la rage des dents.*

Early recipes are precise about the kind of sour wine (*vin aigre*) to be used and the time taken over the grinding of the seeds. From the mid seventeenth century '*statuts et ordonnances*' were set up in an attempt to ensure quality, and the Confrérie des Vinaigriers, under their patron saint, Vincent, was established and became as influential as any similar organization associated with wine or with olive oil. By the late nineteenth century various manufacturers existed, but while Dijon (and its major rival Meaux to the north) remains the traditional centre of the French mustard industry, Moutarde de Dijon is made throughout the world. Still unique, however, and much in demand by collectors, are the original glazed earthenware (*faïence*) mustard pots with their regal designs from the eighteenth and early nineteenth centuries.

By comparison with *pain d'épice* and mustard, which have a proud history from the Middle Ages, *cassis*, the liqueur made from blackcurrants, has a relatively recent one. The medicinal and remedial properties of the berries were supposed to be even more wide-ranging than those of mustard. According to the Abbé Bailly in the early eighteenth century they not only cured indigestion but fevers and smallpox as well. The juice, heated and inhaled, prevented colds and cleared the brain, and was certainly the most effective treatment for an upset liver or spleen. The qualities of *ribes nigrum* have been recognized by much more recent specialists, especially in the treatment of circulatory problems. Another, more popular use of the leaves, still practiced in many country areas of France today, is to rub them on insect stings. It is certainly effective.

Although as a drink *cassis* is known to have existed in the north of France it appears not to have been exploited on any scale until the mid nineteenth century, while the official recognition according by the *appellation* 'Cassis de Dijon' was not awarded until 1923. But production is now, by any standards, phenomenal. The label of L'Héritier-Guyot on a bottle signifies the major producer. In the factory in the north-east suburbs of Dijon nearly half of France's total production is made from a harvest of around 5000 tonnes of fruit per year! Much of this in France and abroad is used in the drink *vin blanc cassis* which, in keeping with strict tradition, should be made with one third *liqueur de cassis* and two thirds of *aligoté*, the wine from the commonest white wine grape in Burgundy. I find the L'Héritier-Guyot product perfectly acceptable, as do many of my French friends, but it is always worth inquiring when you are tasting wine if there is any *cassis* for sale locally. If you are lucky you will be able to buy a bottle of home-produced, deeply flavoured *cassis* rarely found in any shop. (Although produced on quite a large scale, the one on sale in the Caves Ligourneau in the village of Gamay is a reliable purchase.) The drink existed for many years but it owes its name (since 1951) to Mayor Félix Kir and is customarily served as an aperitif. (*'Un petit kir?'* must be the most frequently proposed pre-dinner drink in all of France.) But it too has suffered from exploitation. 'Kir' may now be purchased pre-mixed from the supermarket shelf and it has become increasingly fashionable to blend *aligoté* with *mûre* (blackberry) or *framboise* (raspberry). *'Kir royal'* is a mixture of blackcurrant and sparkling wine. Possibly by analogy with the fashion for mixing drinks in this way, *cassis* and red wine are also served. This is known as *un communard* after the Paris Commune of 1871, a reference to its political colour.

Like so many French provincial towns of its size, Dijon is easily and indeed best explored on foot and there is no better place to begin than the Palais des Ducs. Opposite, across the Rue de la Liberté, is the semi-circular Place de la Libération, bounded on its southern side by a graceful crescent designed in the late seventeenth century by one of Versailles' architects, Jules Hardouin-Mansart, who was also responsible for the Place des Victoires in central Paris. Originally the Place Royale, it was dominated by an equestrian statue of Louis XIV which became one of the victims of the Revolutionaries' zeal a century later. Today the Place de la Libération (so named since 1944) is a busy car-park and the crescent contains a range of expensive shops, but it is easy to imagine how elegant it must once have been.

Having designed the Place Royale, Hardouin-Mansart then turned his attention to the palace. Of the original buildings which had belonged to the Capetian dukes virtually nothing remained, and what he had to work on were those that had been built from the Valois dynasty. By the early nineteenth century the palace existed as we can see it today. Behind wrought-iron railings, the *cour d'honneur* is surrounded on three sides by bare, classically severe façades. To the west and east covered passages lead to inner courtyards, the Cour de Flore and the Cour de Bar. The latter is dominated by a square tower 46 metres high of the same name, built by Philippe le Hardi as a look-out post and so called for having once served for six years (1431–7) as a prison for the Duc de Bar who later became the Roi René of Provence. At the foot of the tower in the attractive little Place des Ducs is a staircase leading to an elegant enclosed gallery and a statue by Henri Bouchard of the Dutch sculptor Claus Sluter (who designed Philippe le Hardi's tomb, now in the Musée des Beaux Arts), meaningfully clutching his hammer and chisel. Opposite the tower are the original kitchens of the palace, a reminder of a more ordinary, if necessary, aspect of an aristocratic régime. None of the original equipment remains, but the ingenuity of its design, especially its six hearths, the way it is lit and was intended to be ventilated, is remarkable.

The kitchens have long served in recent years as a reception room for public functions and are now part of the Musée des Beaux Arts, constructed in the mid nineteenth century and considered to house one of the richest collections in France. The entrance is in the Place de la Sainte Chapelle and the staircase to the immediate right leads directly to the Gallerie Bellegarde and in turn to the sumptuous Salle des Gardes. When I first visited this museum many years ago in order specifically to see the ducal tombs I arrived late, only minutes before the official closing time. My enthusiasm and genuine frustration were evident, and the officials not only allowed me in and delayed closing the museum, but refused to take any entrance fee! Nowhere else in a public building in France have I met with such generosity and patience.

To attempt to describe the collection housed in the museum even in general terms would require much time and space and would do it scant justice. Overall it is especially rewarding for anyone interested in the development of Burgundian art and of a local Dijon school as well, but magnificent examples of French, Swiss, German, Dutch and Spanish painting and sculpture from the Middle Ages to the present fill room after room. As in so many museums, there are also many pieces which, for reasons of fragility or quality, are not on display. These include examples of Egyptian and Oriental work which can in fact usually be seen on request, especially if the museum is not busy. But no reference to the collection should fail to mention the Donation Granville. Pierre Granville, one-time theatre director and art journalist for *Le Monde*, and Kathleen Parker made several bequests to the museum from 1969 to the late 1980s, including works by Delacroix, Géricault and Picasso. Granville became director of the museum and personally supervised with striking success the redesigning of the rooms in which this collection is to be found.

The focal point of the museum is, of course, the Salle des Gardes, the one-time main room of the ducal palace. It has been restored and reworked over the centuries but has retained its ornate, monumental fireplace and has a small gallery, from which there is a fine view down on the tombs of the first two Valois dukes, brought here in 1827 from the Chartreuse de Champmol.

With an eye to posthumous glory, Philippe le Hardi commissioned his tomb and saw the first designs prepared by Claus Sluter before his death in 1404. The result, albeit much restored, is an extraordinary mixture of grace, splendour and grief. The duke's effigy, in a white robe and a blue cape fringed with gold, his feet resting on a lion and his hands in a gesture of prayer, lies on a black marble slab. Two angels with delicate golden wings hold a bonnet at his head. Around the tomb is its most celebrated feature, a series of miniature cloisters filled with forty *pleurants* (mourners) in alabaster. These tiny, delicately carved figures, some fat, some thin, and including two children, are clad in robes, most with their hoods pulled down over their head as a sign of mourning. But a few have their faces exposed and Sluter (or his nephew Claus de Werve, who took over the work after his uncle's death in 1406) has captured their expressions of deep sorrow in a wholly realistic way.

The second tomb, that of Jean sans Peur and his wife Marguerite de Bavière, was designed and built over fifty years later. The work was carried out by a Spaniard, Juan de la Huerta, and Antoine le Moiturier from Avignon, and both time and different artistic traditions have left their mark. This later tomb is more ornate. The canopies of the arcades are more elaborate, angels clutch musical instruments and look decidedly less sorrowful. But the colours are just as splendid, and together these two tombs somehow sum up the magnificence of a remarkable dynasty. And if this were not enough the Salle des Gardes also contains several altar-pieces and tapestries. Two of the altar-pieces in particular are sumptuous and were commissioned by Philippe le Hardi for the Chartreuse. The first, which dates from the very end of the fourteenth century, has the crucifixion as its central subject but contains other scenes from Christ's life; the second represents various saints and martyrs. Both are remarkable for the quality of their decorative work rather than for any expression of religious fervour. But the first is especially notable for what is claimed to be the only extant example of painting and gilding by Melchior Broederlam, Philippe le Hardi's court painter.

Less than 100 metres to the north of the Palais des Ducs, and dominating the medieval area of the town, is the church of Notre-Dame. It is best approached by the Rue de la Chouette, which takes you past the early seventeenth-century Hôtel de Vogüé, whose italianate arched doorway topped by an elaborately carved panel leads to an inner courtyard. Many consider this to be the most elegant house in Dijon and it may not be entirely without coincidence that it is occupied by the town's architectural offices. Next door is the sixteenth-century Maison Millière, with attractive timber-work, including an original main beam on which the initials of the various owners are carved.

If you stand in the Rue de la Chouette and observe passers-by, you will notice that many reach up to touch, making a wish as they do so, the small effigy of an owl (after which the street is named) carved in the north wall of the church. Various stories are told about its significance. One in particular claims that it symbolizes the Jews who preferred the darkness to the light of the Gospels and had been cast out by the Christian Church. But there is a more homely and popular version. This tells how an owl with a broken leg was discovered by the architect of Notre-Dame when he first arrived in Dijon. He cared for it until it recovered, after which it continued to visit him in his workshop. Part of his task was to decorate the west façade of the church, both with gargoyles representing the vices and sins which people would leave behind as they entered, and with designs based on local flowers. The architect was too busy to go out and observe people or collect plants and so the owl went for him. He would return each evening and the architect would draw what it had seen. During the night it would set off again in search of leaves and stalks with the result that there was no longer any time for it to sleep. Eventually the church was finished. A mass was held to consecrate it which the architect attended carrying the owl in his pocket. After the mass he was going to put it on his shoulder as was his custom but found that it had died from exhaustion. Saddened beyond belief, the architect made a tiny coffin for it and sealed it in the north wall of Notre-Dame. Then he carved the bird's effigy on the outside.

Notre-Dame is a gem and thought by many to be a cathedral in miniature, somehow squashed into the busiest part of the town. The interior is light and elegant in typical Burgundian Gothic style, especially the choir, where the vaulted roof appears to rest on the slenderest of columns. Though the church has been damaged over the centuries, some fragments of fine stained glass from the thirteenth century can be seen in the north transept, as well as some original carving. South of the choir, draped in a golden cloak, is the primitive statue of the Black Virgin that was paraded before the besieging armies in 1513. The marks in her apron are said to have been caused by Swiss bullets, and the adoration she continues to attract today is clearly witnessed by the large number of *ex-votos* nearby. But if the interior of Notre-Dame is attractive, the west façade is quite startling. Above the three arches (badly mutilated at the time of the Revolution) spanning the full width of the church are two rows of sixteen blind arcades, divided by slim columns. These three main sections are separated horizontally by friezes decorated with floral designs and with sixteen false gargoyles, many of which have hideously distorted faces, anticipating by several centuries the work of Picasso (it has been said) and, perhaps even more strikingly, Francis Bacon's *Figures at the Base of a Crucifixion*. The owl's work was well done.

The west façade also has one other special feature. Its southern tower bears a clock known as the *jacquemart*, brought to Dijon in 1382 by Philippe le Hardi as part of his booty after defeating the Flemish, who had risen in rebellion against his uncle Charles

VI. By the seventeenth century a female figure was added, and during the next two hundred years two 'children'. The clock now strikes every quarter hour and is held in as much affection by the *dijonnais* as the architect's owl.

To return to the Place de la Libération, skirting the western end of the Palais des Ducs, takes only a few minutes. But the few adjoining streets are worth exploring for the numerous houses built for the growing numbers of the new *noblesse de robe* between the fifteenth and late eighteenth centuries. Of particular note is the late fifteenth century Hôtel Chambellan, now the local tourist office, in the Rue des Forges. Behind the rather blank and functional front lies a splendid courtyard with an inner stairway and double balcony. The Hôtel Bonhier-de-Lantenay, in the Rue de la Préfecture, built three centuries later, has housed the local regional offices since the early nineteenth century. Few civil servants have more elegant surroundings in which to work. And if the onslaught of history is overwhelming, the chemist's shop specializing in homoeopathic medicines and natural treatment in the Rue Musette is well worth a visit for its arrays of porcelain apothecary jars — another reminder of the Dijonnais' claims for their healthy environment.

Just as impressive as the splendid town houses in and around the Rue de la Préfecture are those to the south of the Place de la Libération leading to the Palais de Justice and just beyond to the town library. One in particular, the Hôtel Legouz-de-Gerland in the Rue J. B. Liégeard, ranks with the best of Dijon's domestic architecture. The original house here was built in the fifteenth century, but owes many of its present features to work carried out three hundred years later under the supervision of the Legouz family. The semi-circular courtyard with its balustrade consciously echoing the nearby Place de la Libération, the two pairs of lions guarding what were once the stables and the magnificent sculpted doorways, and the family initials carved into the lintels above the windows looking on to the courtyard are just some of the impressive reminders of a special social status. Equally imposing is the Hôtel Bouhier-de-Savigny in Rue Vauban, with its monumental doorway and staircase. It was the birthplace in 1693 of Jean Bouhier, who became President of the Dijon parliament and a member of the French Academy; his portrait hangs in the Musée des Beaux-Arts. But there are signs here too of more intimate matters. A small sculpted cat impassively observing passers-by is a motif from the coat of arms of a later owner, Micault de Courbeton, and fake painted windows remind us that even the wealthy chose to avoid the tax levied on doors and windows in the early nineteenth century.

Dominating this part of the town is the Palais de Justice. Here Dijon's *parlement* – really the High Court – was established by Louis XII after the end of the Valois dynasty, and is still used today for certain judicial hearings. The outside is not particularly impressive but the main room, the Salle des Pas-Perdus, is vast (39 metres long), with a barrel-vault ceiling. Before the Revolution this was used as a market and it is said that stall-holders regularly did a good trade with the lawyers and magistrates, who seemed more interested in striking a bargain than in their professional duties.

From the Palais de Justice the Rue Amiral Roussin leads to the town library, famous for its collection of illuminated Cistercian manuscripts from the abbey at Cîteaux. Such is their fragility that they are not allowed to be shown publicly, but there are high-quality reproductions. To the south of the library is the Rue du Petit Potet, which marks the point where the Suzon flowed into the ditch around the medieval town. Cellars here are still affected by damp (*potet* meant swamp). This area can be reached by way of the narrow Rue Hernoux which leads to the Place des Cordeliers, a reminder of the order of Franciscans with their rope belts. Near by, linking the Rue Pasteur to the Rue Chabot-Charny, is the Rue du Prieuré, formerly known as the Cour d'Époisses, a name which has nothing unusual about it. But it is still just possible to see, carved in the stone above the present name-plate, 'Cour des Poisses'. 'Poisses' meant prostitutes and it is held locally that the name had to be altered since so many nuns frequented this part of town!

West from the Place des Cordeliers takes you to the other cluster of buildings which formed part of medieval Dijon, around the cathedral of Saint-Bénigne and the Church of Saint-Philibert. The streets here have been subject to considerable restoration. Of particular interest and attraction are the Rue Monge and the Rue Condorcet. These streets for long provided access to a crossing point on the Ouche, and many of the buildings are said to have been inns catering for the traffic, with the result that there is a distinctly more popular or more homely atmosphere about them even today. However, both have houses once again recalling the elegance of the seventeenth and eighteenth centuries.

The northern end of the Rue Condorcet runs into the square to the south of the cathedral by the west door of Saint-Philibert, and in fact crosses the vast cemetery which was once here. (Tombs are still discovered in the course of restoration work in the area today.) Saint-Philibert began in the ninth century as a chapel for the novices attached to Saint-Bénigne and, much developed, assumed its present name three centuries later on becoming the church of the poorest parish in Dijon. Its history has been uneasy. After the Revolution it was used to stable horses, and later in the nineteenth century it became a storehouse for salt, which caused severe damage to the stonework. It is now in a poor, even dangerous condition and the inside may not be visited unless you have special permission. Such deterioration can only be regretted since the church is clearly attractive and the only complete Romanesque building in Dijon. (The stone spire and belfry were added in the sixteenth century.) Still, it is to be hoped that the main entrance with its carvings, elegant columns and capitals, and the remains of a fifteenth-century fresco of the crucifixion may encourage the authorities to consider a total restoration which, however expensive, would be immensely worthwhile.

Towering above Saint-Philibert is Saint-Bénigne, built on the site of no less than five churches in honour of the patron saint, which became the cathedral when, in 1731, Dijon became the seat of an independent bishopric. Of the present building, the earliest part dates from the very end of the tenth century when William of Volpiano came from Italy to begin work on an entire monastery, of which parts can still be seen in the rotunda at the east end of the church and in the nearby archaeological museum.

From early records and descriptions Volpiano's church, completed around 1020, must have been magnificent. The chronicler Raoul Glaber described it as the 'most marvellous basilica' in the entire country, an assessment which modern archaeologists' plans certainly support. One hundred metres long, it incorporated a great nave with double side aisles, a crossing, choir and apse with three altars and surrounded by an ambulatory flanked with pillars. But the church's outstanding feature, acknowledged by all historians, was its rotunda. Clearly Italian in origin, it was built on three levels, the top two being subsequently destroyed at the Revolution. This form of construction was a reflection upwards of the three concentric circles of pillars (eight, sixteen and twenty-four respectively) on the bottom level. Although the present rotunda was much restored, using material from the upper levels, in 1843, the effect is impressive. You enter what Robert Speaight in a happy phrase described as a 'forest of pillars, stout as the oaks of the Morvan'; it is also as shadowy and mysterious. The capitals on these pillars, many of them primitive, have long been a matter of speculation and debate. The most famous one is of a man with monstrous hands raised in adoration (or in fear?), but others, of animals or mysterious creatures and plants, are like remnants of a bad dream. What precisely their origins are is not decided. Some experts claim the influence of Islamic art, others simply evidence of hurried restorative work. More probable is the explanation that, like similar figures in Saint-Philibert in Tournus, they are examples of Burgundian decorative religious art in its earliest form. There remains nonetheless something distinctively pagan and even primeval about them.

However magnificent Volpiano's building may have been, it did not last for long. In 1137 a fire destroyed much of it and nearly 150 years later in 1272 the tower collapsed into the main body of the church. Restoration was the work of Hugues d'Arc and Saint-Bénigne today is one of the region's principal illustrations of Burgundian Gothic architecture. Such is the historical interest of the rotunda, however, and indeed of the whole of Volpiano's original group of monastic buildings, that Hugues' church can be neglected. Admittedly there is something rather bleak about it which seems to come from more than just the rather severe design, due, some have claimed, to the small budget with which Hugues had to work. And yet features such as the tall windows in the clerestory or the choir are individually elegant and attractive. Perhaps the impression is brought in from the outside. Due presumably to a lack of space, the flying buttresses which lighten the aspect of even the most massive of cathedrals (Notre-Dame in Paris, for example) have had to be discarded in favour of solid buttresses, which cut through the upward thrusting movement normally characteristic of this style. Alongside the delicacy of Saint-Philibert, Saint-Bénigne seems heavy indeed.

Just to the north of the cathedral is Dijon's archaeological museum, containing relics from the earliest periods of the region's history: palaeolithic and neolithic tools and implements, bronze-age jewellery, including a collection from the village of Blanot which was literally unearthed when a storm blew down an oak tree in 1982, and Gallo-Roman and Merovingian artefacts of all kinds. All of these exhibits are attractively displayed in the place where originally monks had their individual cells. On the ground floor, formerly the dormitory of the monastery, are pieces of Romanesque sculpture and some work by Sluter, including a moving bust of Christ which originally formed part of the Puits de Moïse at the Chartreuse de Champmol. Beneath these, in what was the abbey's chapter-house, we find relics from the Gallo-Roman period. Attention is drawn in particular to a bronze statue of Sequana, the goddess of the Seine, discovered during excavations at the source of the river where her sanctuary contained thousands of *ex-votos* representing the parts of the body from which believers were suffering. Carved in bronze, stone and even in wood, they witness a highly popular cult which was developing in the first years of Christianity in the region. But while these and rows of funerary statues and slabs of various dignitaries are impressive, especially touching is one of a wine merchant serving a customer, surrounded by his various measures and pieces of equipment. This, like the incomplete slab alongside depicting a butcher, is a reminder of everyday life as it was centuries ago.

The sheer size of the rooms in which this rich collection is housed is evidence of the extent of Volpiano's original abbey. Most of the rest has disappeared, but in the nearby Rue de la Prévoté is a detail which should not be missed. Here at no. 4 is a large reception room belonging to the Hôtel du Chapeau-Rouge in the Rue Michelet. It has apparently served as a shop and as a garage but for centuries it was used by the monks to store their wine — monastic life was not always dreary.

Directly west from the Place Saint-Bénigne, a twenty-minute walk takes you past the Jardin de l'Arquebuse, where Dijon's botanic gardens can be visited, to the Chartreuse de Champmol. Now a psychiatric hospital, this is where Philippe le Hardi had a monastery built, beyond the walls of the medieval city, as a burial place for the dukes of the Valois dynasty. After nearly five centuries most of the Chartreuse was destroyed at the time of the Revolution, when it was sold as building materials. Only the original chapel doorway (incorporated into a nineteenth-century church) and the Puits de Moïse remain, both essentially the work of Sluter. The former in particular is a fine example of his dramatic, realistic work. Philippe, looking appropriately self-satisfied, and his wife Marguerite are shown praying to the Virgin Mary, but what is most striking is the statue of the baby Jesus, already anxiously eyeing the instruments of the Passion. The Puits de Moïse is — or was — a more ambitious venture, carved at the end of his career. It originally stood in an ornamental pond in the centre of the monastery's great cloister, and celebrated water as the source of all life. What remains is only the lower part (the bust of Christ is in the museum), containing giant figures of Old Testament prophets whose faces were inspired, it is said, by those of the Jewish people Sluter saw around him in Dijon. Each holds a scroll bearing an inscription foretelling Christ's Passion, and each is given distinctive, individual features. As you can see from a few traces which remain, they were originally coloured and gilded, and to increase the realism of his work Sluter provided David's harp with metal strings and Jeremiah with a pair of spectacles. All of this can be inspected at close range. The Puits is protected from the weather by a kind of greenhouse and there is a raised walkway around the statues. Plans have been approved — and money found — to pull down the nearby modern buildings and create a garden having the dimensions of the original cloister, and to restore the statues to their original position.

Apart from these two examples of Sluter's skill, there is not much else of historic interest to be seen, but you may walk at will through the grounds, which are wooded and carefully tended.

There is an atmosphere of quiet care, probably rather different today from what it must have been in 1843 when the Chartreuse was re-opened as the '*asile départemental des aliénés*'.

On returning to the town centre, few places offer more pleasant surroundings for refreshments and from which to watch the Dijonnais go about their business than the Jardin Darcy or one of the cafés around the nearby Place. Here you have an unspoiled example of late nineteenth- and early twentieth-century elegance, as far a cry from the dingy, threatening streets of the Middle Ages as from the inhospitable town which Henry Miller thought he had found. Dijon has come a long way. I recall once discussing the rivalry between Dijon and Beaune with the owner of a small hotel. She could hardly have been more dismissive: 'The *hospices* and wine, yes – but the rest . . . And in any case Beaune is *very* small.' Dijon has, without doubt, established itself as the capital of Burgundy and as one of the central and most vibrant provincial towns of the new western Europe.

3
The Golden Trail

As I have already claimed in the Introduction, for many if not most people Burgundy is virtually limited to that strip of land which has given its name to the *département* as a whole, the Côte d'Or. This narrow tract of wine country about 60 kilometres long runs alongside the N74 south of Dijon to Beaune and then, as it broadens out, to just north of Chalon-sur-Saône. At its narrowest it is barely a couple of kilometres wide; at its widest, around Chagny, perhaps ten. Quite where the name comes from is uncertain, but the general view is that it suggests the autumnal colours of the landscape. Certainly when the grapes are harvested in late September or early October the description is justified, though reds and bronze are much in evidence too. Most of the wine is produced from the vines grown (on average at an altitude of around 250 metres) on the lower flanks of the hills or La Côte rising up on the west side of the N74. Scarcely a year passes, however, without some ambitious (or greedy) *vigneron* carving out a new patch of land from the wooded tops of the hills.

When precisely wine was first produced here is not known. The Romans had found vines growing here when they arrived, but it seems likely that the earliest serious cultivation for the purposes of making wine dates from the Middle Ages and was something which developed around the great monasteries. The monks from Cîteaux, for example, are known to have cultivated the Clos de Vougeot from the twelfth century. The present richness of the area is relatively modern, however. What vines there were in the nineteenth century were seriously attacked (as were those in the south-west of France too) by phylloxera, and only careful tending and grafting enabled many of them to survive. But with that disease now far less of a threat, the only real problems are from the vagaries of the weather. Even so the situation is ideal. The vines are protected from prevailing westerly winds and spring frosts, they benefit from morning sun and enjoy an efficient natural irrigation. Some are grown as well to the east of the N74, particularly just beyond Dijon, but the land here as it stretches away to the wetter parts of the valley of the Saône is more suitable for fruit orchards and grain. For the production of good wine the right kind of climate is essential. Ideally the winters should be relatively dry, with light rain in June and July followed by a ripening sun. The dangers are from rapid and extreme changes of temperature, frost and hailstorms. At the same time climate and soil have to be complemented by knowledge, skill and hard work. After the *vendange*, the harvest, the vines are cleaned and pruned, and the soil carefully treated. During the winter the soil is further dressed and general maintenance of the vineyards is carried out: the restaking and rewiring of the vines, or repairs to the surrounding walls. On steep slopes, topsoil washed down by the year's rain will be laboriously carried back up as well. In the spring, perhaps the most critical time of all, the vines are pruned again, the ground cleaned and a careful watch kept out for insects and disease, notably rot. This can be cold work and the piles of smouldering cuttings (*sarments*) provide not only a pleasant scent but patches of welcome warmth for the workers. Much of the work is slow, tedious and lonely, and at the end of a cold winter day the atmosphere of geniality in a local café is an interesting and instructive experience.

It is not all that long ago that horses were used and the rows of vines had to be planted wide enough apart to allow machinery to pass between them. Nowadays the *enjambeur*, a tractor with wheels high enough to bridge the vines, allows for more intensive growing and easier working conditions. New vines, too, demand constant attention. With high land prices the investment required is considerable and there is no return for at least four years.

And even when harvested the grapes need the attention born of generations of experience. Methods and equipment vary very considerably. Some of the bigger properties have their stainless steel vats and computerized programmes, but others have retained traditional methods and owners will be delighted to show you their wine in its different stages of maturing. They can also be extraordinarily reluctant to sell older vintages, as though to part with even three or four bottles is physically a painful experience. Many *caves* are prepared for the passing tourist, with seats cut from barrels, maps of the region on the walls, corkscrews made from gnarled pieces of vine for sale and reminders that wine is better for you than water. If you are fortunate enough to get to know a grower slightly off the main route, or whose production is really small and for which he has a guaranteed local market, you will have the impression of a way of life not fully touched by the twentieth century. There is rivalry and envy between growers but immense pride in achievements and, once you have shown yourself to be genuinely interested and, better still, equipped with a little knowledge, they will talk about their wine and introduce you to it with infectious enthusiasm. The very real curiosity of one grower I know in Fixin, who works his vineyards with his son, is reflected in a collection of single bottles of wines in his principal cellar from all over the world. And yet while he admits readily enough that his is only a *petit vin* by comparison with many made locally, he defends it to the end. And rightly so. At the same time for every honest grower there is probably one who is less so. The blending of wines has long been traditional in Burgundy, and in this area especially of red wine. The *passe-tout-grains* is a standard and quite legitimate mixture of the Pinot Noir and Gamay grapes. Merchants may buy their wines from different growers and then blend them — this will almost always be the case in a wine whose name includes *villages* on the label as, for example, in Côte de Beaune Villages. Mixing with wine from other areas, however, is illegal, but it exists and the situation has been created, largely, by market forces. Production in Burgundy by comparison with, say, the Bordeaux area, is small, but demand is high, especially from the Swiss, the Germans and, interestingly, the Scandinavians. Not infrequently, second-rate wine is fortified by blending it with wines brought in from the Rhône vineyards to the south or even from Algeria or Italy. While legislation and the application of the *appellation contrôlée* are there in principle to protect the customer, they are not always as strictly enforced as they might be. Nonetheless, whatever the practice, the list of the great wine areas is impressive and seductive: the Côte de Nuits with Gevrey Chambertin, Vosne-Romanée and Vougeot; the Côte de Beaune with Aloxe-Corton, Pommard, Meursault, Chassagne- and Puligny-Montrachet; the Côte Chalonnaise with Mercurey and Givry. But while these are the main divisions and best known *crus*, there are dozens of others. In the Côte de Nuits, centred on Nuits-Saint-Georges, for example, perhaps the most intensively worked of all, there are about thirty different *appellations contrôlées*. And even a single *grand cru* coming from a vineyard like the Clos du Chapître in Fixin or the Clos de Vougeot will be subdivided into several, even dozens of separate plots, owned by different people. A good way to see how all these vines are divided out is to leave the main road and wander at random along the tracks used by the vineyard workers. Not only do you then see how small some of these plots are, you will also notice how individual growers have their own particular methods: some will prune their vines a week earlier than others, some will spray with sulphates in a different way, some experiment with growing grass between the vines in an attempt to reduce as far as possible soil erosion and to retain humidity. How to choose what to buy and where obviously depends to a large extent on knowledge, but for the average non-specialist *amateur de vin* luck as much as advice is necessary. In broad terms the wines of the Côte de Nuits are heavier, more pungent and darker than those further south. But, while different in flavour, a red from Marsannay may be as light in body as one from Chagny, 60 kilometres away. Local hotels or restaurants are often a good source of information, but if you do accept any of the many invitations to a roadside *dégustation* – even to one of the larger, more prestigious châteaux or *clos* – do not be afraid to leave empty-handed if you do not like what you have sampled.

If you head for the vines south of Dijon it is striking how quickly the town 'disappears'. Certainly the village of Chenôve has its share of commuter housing and seems more an extended suburb of Dijon than a village. Yet it remains celebrated for the huge fifteenth-century wine presses made for the Ducs de Valois which, we are told, were still in regular use less than a hundred years ago. Then, by the time you reach the village of Marsannay, within 2 kilometres, the vine has asserted itself and you sense you have entered a different kind of society. To have the best impression of this extraordinarily intensively cultivated area, however, it is advisable to avoid Dijon altogether and approach Marsannay from the exit on the A38 motorway opposite Velars-sur-Ouche. The road climbs steeply through thick forests of oaks, beech, birch, chestnut and conifers, eventually reaching a junction marked by a cross and a sign to Mont Afrique (where there is a communications tower), the high point of the Côte at 584 metres. The road continues up to this but a clearly marked path allows you to walk round the summit and provides you with some impressive panoramic views over Dijon and also eastwards to the Saône. Although there is no particular path marked, it is also possible from here to cut north-west through the forest to join the Grande Randonnée 7, and thence north to the statue of Notre Dame d'Étang. This marks the spot where in the fifteenth century a statue of the Virgin Mary (now in the village church) is said to have been discovered. Again there are splendid views, especially following the line of the Grande Randonnée 7 northwards across the Ouche and to the forests of Pasques and Val-Suzon. The road then drops down through a series of tight bends to the vineyards, though first you have to cross a military exercise ground which is sometimes closed – and that can be infuriating since the only other way by car is across the southern edge of Dijon. With its mixture of fruit trees (especially cherries) and vines, Marsannay is pretty. Here what is arguably the best *vin rosé* in the whole of Burgundy is to be found, especially that produced by the Domaine Clair-Daü, where some walls of the buildings once formed parts of the chapel of the Bishops of Langres. Against one of them are two quite splendid vines, said to be over 400 years old and still producing magnificent bunches of grapes. After Marsannay the *route des grands crus* (D122) provides a leisurely and, in spring or summer, agreeable way to explore as far as Vougeot. But, as I have already suggested, it is worth leaving even this minor road for the tracks which cut back and forth across the vineyards. And while it is especially pleasant in the warmth of the summer, to do so in winter is an altogether different experience. Against a dusting of snow on the ground the vines, severely pruned, form a stark, skeletal pattern and give no indication of the beauty that will appear several months later.

At Fixin the Côte de Nuits officially begins. Like all of the small villages it is immaculate. Clean stone houses, some with inner courtyards, reflect not only prosperity but a simple, quiet pride. The traditional house has an outside stair (usually covered nowadays) giving access to the living area. The most elegant ones often have a small first-floor terrace as well. On the ground floor are storerooms, workrooms and often a cellar where bottled wine is housed. Beneath are the cellars proper, dark and musty, where the vine is busily maturing (or working – *travailler* – as the French say) in oak casks and where the *vigneron* will come from time to time to test, judging the precise moment when he must move it on to the next stage. As you walk up the hill from the village centre you pass the small fourteenth-century church with its square tower and pyramid shaped roof. Inside is a remarkably well-preserved coloured picture on wood of the Madonna and Child which is a century older. Beyond is the Clos de Napoléon and a fourteenth-century manor house. This tribute to the Emperor is not by chance. One of Napoleon's captains, Claude Noiset, retired to Fixin after the Battle of Waterloo and as a tribute to his leader had the celebrated sculptor François Rude create a statue to his memory. This 'Réveil de Napoléon' (1847) depicts the emperor wakening to take his place amongst the immortals. Leading up to the statue are a hundred steps, recalling the celebrated 'Hundred Days'. Some of the detail of the statue is strikingly delicate, as on the handle of his sword, for example. Such was Noiset's admiration that he asked to be buried upright facing his hero, but, it is said, the grave diggers found the rock too hard to dig that deep! Noiset also had a small house built in the woods which is now a museum. Its rather ornate crenellations – out of place in this lovely setting – are an echo of the tenth-century fortifications on the island of Elba. Once you have climbed the hundred steps and paid your respects to the recumbent figure, you should continue up and over the hill by way of any of the colour-coded paths joining, if you wish, the Grande

Randonnée 7. Within three to four hours you can bear south to the hamlet of Chamboeuf and then follow the road (D31) down the Combe de Lavaux with its jagged limestone outcrops into Gevrey Chambertin and back to Fixin.

Gevrey Chambertin itself has all kinds of echoes from a Roman and medieval past and boasts one of the most celebrated wine names in Europe. From here to Vougeot the vineyards have nearly all, at some time or another, belonged to or been worked by the Cistercian community at Cîteaux, access to which is provided by various small roads leading east from the N74 through vines at first and then across fields of cereal crops and thick woods. The land is flat and damp. Irrigation channels are much in evidence and the abbey is surrounded by the Vouge and its tributaries. With few exceptions, notably a fifteenth-century library and copying room both undergoing restoration, the buildings were almost entirely destroyed at the Revolution and the present ones date from the nineteenth century. A hundred and fifty years ago the abbey became a prison or remand home for young offenders and during the two World Wars was used as a hospital. Today Cîteaux is a working monastery (the monks farm, or study in the library) and the public are not admitted except to a small entrance hall where a video display provides a rather pedestrian account of the community's history and describes the modern monk's daily routine. The original abbey was established here at the very end of the eleventh century by Robert de Molesmes, whose task was to develop a rule that was simple and of true Benedictine inspiration, in contrast to what was seen as the increasingly free interpretation of the order's teaching by the monks at Cluny. Like most Cistercian abbeys — Le Thoronet or Silvacane further south in Provence, or Morimondo in Lombardy for example — Cîteaux is situated on a low spot, in recognition of true humility. Its name derives probably from *cistelli* or rushes, and even with modern building techniques and materials it must be a damp, cold place in the middle of November when the mists swirl about its walls.

While their choice of site may well have had something to do with Christian humility, the early monks at Cîteaux soon acquired the *clos* at Vougeot and continued to cultivate it for the best part of 700 years. By the end of the twelfth century they had built themselves all that was necessary to make wine (though they employed specialist cellarmen) and today the four huge original presses, made from local oak, can be admired in the *cuverie*, which is curiously more like a cloister than a true working area. The whole complex of buildings at Vougeot has undergone much restoration and the *cellier*, with its narrow windows, is much used today for banquets and receptions. (The meals and wines served can be truly gargantuan and impressive . . .) Even so the original atmosphere remains and has been exploited by the Confrérie des Chevaliers du Tastevin. Founded in 1934, this organization was essentially a commercial venture, whatever *mystique* some local people will attempt to attribute to it. Membership is bought rather than earned, and the qualification is in no way an indication of any knowledge of wine. People from all over the world arrive at the château, purchased by the Confrérie in 1944, to participate in the ceremonies, and to be tapped on the shoulder with a piece of vine and enrolled with the words: '*Par Noé père de la vigne, par Bacchus dieu du vin, par saint Vincent patron des vignerons, nous vous armons chevalier du Tastevin!*'. Yet for all its commercial hype and harmless nonsense, some serious tasting is undertaken at Vougeot, traditionally on the last Saturday before Palm Sunday weekend. As a result of this, successful wines are permitted to bear the description of '*tastevinés*'; it is an assessment reflected in the price. In fact, in view of the kind of rating usually accorded to Clos de Vougeot wines, a word of caution may not be amiss. It has long been established that the subsoil here is more varied than that of any other *grand cru* in Burgundy. Furthermore, problems of drainage result in the lower areas of the *clos* being distinctly inferior to those higher up. Even more interesting is the fact that the 50 hectares of vines are divided between more than seventy different owners, some with plots big enough only to produce a few barrels. Some of these owners do group themselves together into a kind of mini cooperative; others do not, and content themselves with adding the grapes to some other wine, but still use (and benefit from) Vougeot in a double-barrelled name on the label.

If wine has had a high enough profile by the time you come to leave Vougeot, there is a most picturesque route to be followed before arriving at Nuits-Saint-Georges. A narrow road skirts the north side of the Clos and climbs up the Combe Ambin to around 500 metres to Reulle-Vergy. According to a model in the local church, Reulle was completely walled in the seventeenth century, and had no fewer than fourteen towers, a large keep and a manor house. Of that rather impressive cluster of buildings only the church itself now remains but the present village is a delight. The museum specializes in the area's traditions, history and geography; examples of local fauna and flora are carefully and instructively set out for anyone wishing to spend time here. There is a marked nature trail leading directly from the museum and, on the first weekend in June, a colourful local crafts fair. From Reulle one road cuts back northwards to Ternant, past two dolmens dating from 2000 BC, and then turns south towards Détain-et-Bruant. This whole area is riddled with caves and underground passages, of which the Grotte de Roche-Chèvre, the Trou du Duc and the Puits Groseille can be visited. Various roads lead back across this beautiful countryside to Nuits, the most attractive of all following the valleys of the Raccordon or the Meuzin. Near by too, just south of Reulle, are the ruins of the monastery of St Vivant, dating from the eleventh century. Old prints show an eighteenth-century monastery in the style of a single-storey château, but by 1800 it was closed and various possessions and materials for building were sold. (The original clock, for example, can now be seen in Prémeaux, just south of Nuits.) The ruins are privately owned but are not properly fenced off, and anyone venturing into them – especially into the cellars – does so at risk.

Nuits-St-Georges suffers from the proximity of both Dijon and Beaune. Once an independent and, in the fourteenth century, a fortified town, it now seems either undecided or overwhelmed. It does of course mark the end of the Côte de Nuits and is still that region's most active commercial centre. It also has its own Hospices wine auction the weekend before Palm Sunday, but even this pales beside the internationally known sales at Beaune. A museum contains some rather sad exhibits of a prehistoric and Gallo-Roman past, and even the twelfth-century Romanesque church of Saint-Symphorien with its typical polychrome tiled roof, generally recognized to be one of the best examples of its kind, seems somehow subdued. There is one unusual link with the modern era, however. In memory of the hero of Jules Verne's novel *Voyage autour de la Lune*, who drinks a bottle of Nuits-Saint-Georges, numerous American astronauts have visited the town. When Apollo XV landed on the moon in 1971 the crew officially baptized one of the craters Cratère Saint-Georges. The terrestrial square now bearing its name was inaugurated two years later.

The demarcation between the Côte de Nuits and the Côte de Beaune is neatly made by the cluster of quarries around Prémeaux and Comblanchien, the latter being derived presumably from *combe blanche*. Although referred to locally as the *marbreries*, these quarries in fact produce a very hard limestone which polishes beautifully, some cream, some tinged with delicate pink. It is found used as far afield as Orly airport, to the south of Paris, as well as the Opéra, Sacré-Coeur and the Gare de Lyon in the capital itself. Comblanchien is also more unhappily noted for the massacre of local people by the Nazis in August 1944 as they fled eastwards pursued by Allied forces.

Within a few kilometres the great wine names begin to reappear – Pernand-Vergelesses and Aloxe-Corton. Few estates can boast a château to rival the latter. It stands on the high north side of the village, its vines spread out in front like a great park. Over the centuries vines here have been owned by the dukes of Burgundy, by the Knights Templar and kings of France; Voltaire is often quoted as saying he preferred the wine from Aloxe-Corton to all others, drinking it in secret himself while giving Beaujolais to his friends. Today that illustrious and romantic past has gone. The château is owned by the famous Louis Latour company and is now used as accommodation for various members of staff and as offices. You are invited to visit the cellars, but the reception – despite a *dégustation* – and display of vineyard tools and cellar equipment are equally indifferent. Not surprisingly it is a prelude to the sales room where your cheque is eagerly awaited.

Rather than rejoin the N74 to reach Beaune it is worth making a small loop west to the neighbouring Savigny-lès-Beaune (*lès* meaning near to). There is a great sweep of valley down south of the village and only a kilometre away the Autoroute du Soleil crosses towards the Beaune junction. The wines here are modest and produced in very large quantities, but the village is renowned for its strange wall inscriptions, carved between the seventeenth and nineteenth centuries. One, reflecting a local pastime, is full of common sense: *'Il ne faut pas donner son appât au goujon quand on peut espérer prendre une carpe'* ('You shouldn't waste your bait on a gudgeon when you hope to catch a carp'). Another is rather more political: *'Travailler est un devoir indispensable à l'homme, riche ou pauvre, puissant ou faible, tout citoyen oisif est un fripon'* ('Every man, rich or poor, powerful or weak, should work; anyone who doesn't is a rogue'). They must be the equivalent of modern-day grafitti, but who wrote them and why is not known. One other more recent event is sometimes recalled by local people. In 1959 a *vigneron*, Paul Dubreuil, who was more interested in wine-making than his vines, spent nearly three weeks in his *cuverie* and nearly asphyxiated himself by the amount of carbon dioxide he inhaled!

Beaune

Although quite a lot of building — commercial as well as domestic — has been allowed outside the walls of Beaune, the local authorities are keen not to have the town expand too far and too fast. Certainly this is reflected in the population, for with just over 20,000 *beaunois* today (barely 12,000 in 1930) it is still only very slightly bigger than it was in the early nineteenth century. Since Dijon had about the same number of people at that time the relative development of the two towns is easily measured. Yet Beaune — or its inhabitants — in no way feels inferior. Rivalry has long been the norm and the smaller town is smugly proud of its attractiveness and reputation.

Beaune's name derives from Belenos, a river god worshipped by the Gauls who established a trading centre here. The Romans also appreciated the strategic potential of the site, and by the fourth century Christianity had arrived. Before they adopted Dijon as their power base ten centuries later the dukes of Burgundy resided here and were responsible for overseeing the construction of most of the town's fortifications. In the late twentieth century, on a major motorway junction and on the main Paris–Lyon railway line, Beaune remains well-placed and could develop (or could have) much more. That it has not reflects the wishes of its inhabitants, but whether it will as decentralization from Paris increases and as communications improve still more remains an interesting question. The people of Beaune tend to be deeply conservative, and in recent years have given hospitality to the summer 'university' run by France's extreme right-wing party, the Front National. But even if that kind of reactionary feeling lies deep, Beaune can hardly afford to be unsympathetic to the crowds of foreigners who flock here during the summer months. One practical consequence of this is a traffic problem. Early in the 1980s much of the town's centre was quite sensibly turned into a pedestrian area, but the result has been to push cars and commercial vehicles on to the ring road. Between June and September – and indeed at certain times of every day throughout the year – this resembles a four- or five-lane racing circuit. Moreover, so bad is the signposting that it is by no means unusual to see cars (and not only foreign ones) circling the town two or three times before their frustrated drivers succeed in finding the exit road they require. It has to be acknowledged, however, that the centre of Beaune has become much more agreeable and that, for those who wish to stop and visit, the car-parking facilities are quite good.

The first impression of Beaune, especially in spring and summer, is of how pretty it is. Immense care is taken over the numerous public gardens and squares, immaculately kept and planted with brightly coloured flowers. The town walls are softened with festoons of greenery and the ditch which once circumvented the town as well has been transformed into gardens and even tennis courts. It is easy to walk round the walls, less than 3 kilometres in length, within an hour or so, and while the presence of traffic is a disturbance it is easy to appreciate how the town looks in upon itself. The original towers and fortified gateways have been modified and the characteristic look-out posts (*échauguettes*) on several were added in the seventeenth century. Several of the towers have become the offices of major wine companies – La Tour Blondeau (Bouchard), La Tour Jolibois (Calvet) and Le Bastion de la Bussière (Patriarche) – and in Le Bastion des Cordeliers are reception rooms for many of Beaune's public functions. While several centuries ago the main gates into the town were Saint-Nicolas to the north and the original castle just to the east, the walls today are breached by a dozen roads, and you quickly find yourself in a concentration of narrow streets, tall houses and private gardens. At the very centre of the town is the church of Notre-Dame, begun early in the twelfth century on the side of the Église Saint-Baudèle which had been destroyed by fire. Although it has been considerably modified, notably in the nineteenth century, the church remains recognizably of Cluniac inspiration and is frequently compared with Saint-Lazare in Autun. But for all its balanced external proportions, what is most attractive and worthwhile about Notre-Dame is to be found inside, notably the carving and works of art. Much of the former depicts standard Christian themes, but those on the capitals to the south side — of grape pickers or of animals playing various musical instruments — are much more realistic in their detail. On the opposite side of the church in the Rolin chapel is a fresco by Pierre Spicre of Lazarus' resurrection which is much admired, and in the choir a part-coloured wooden effigy of the Virgin known as the '*Vierge noire*'. But outstanding among all Burgundian works of art are the five tapestries hung behind the high altar containing nineteen scenes from the life of the Virgin Mary. These too were designed by Spicre in the late fifteenth century and offered to the church by Canon Hugues de Coq, whose generous gesture is commemorated in the final scene in which he can be seen kneeling before Hugues de Cluny. In terms of the story they tell there are some interesting omissions. The absence of both the Marriage of Cana and of Christ's death, for example, is surprising and, as far as I know, has never been explained. But it is not only the narrative content of these tapestries which catches the attention. The workmanship is extraordinarily delicate. The floral patterns in the borders are full of detail, as are the Virgin's facial expressions, but the skill with which colours have been modified makes it appear at times that paint, rather than silk and wool, has been used. One striking example of this is the scene of the Annunciation, in which the angel's garment is transparent and through it we see the stairway just behind him.

Around Notre-Dame are various buildings of note: the fourteenth-century belfry in Place Monge, the ornate sixteenth-century timbered house, the Hôtel de la Rochepot to the east and the attractive Rue de Lorraine beyond with a number of less grand houses from the same period. To the south-west, only a stone's throw from the cloisters, is the Hôtel des Ducs where the Musée du Vin de Bourgogne is housed, opened in 1946 and said to have been the first eco-museum in France. With various kinds of presses, tools and machinery, labels, bottles and tasting-cups it offers a comprehensive collection of items associated with winemaking, but one which seems rather uninspiring in a town which is virtually a *musée du vin* (and a vast cellar) in its own right.

Only 100 metres beyond the museum is Beaune's finest building, the Hôtel-Dieu which dates from 1443. It was conceived by Philippe le Bon's Chancellor, Nicolas Rolin, at a time when Beaune had been ravaged first by famine and then by the plague. For a while Rolin had considered Autun a possibility but having been well received a few years earlier by the people of Beaune he chose the latter. But Rolin was no disinterested philanthropist. Astute, intelligent and thick-skinned, he had made himself a rich man through a series of law suits; he also had an eye for property and he either bought or negotiated the gifting of several plots on which the hospital and its attendant buildings would be built. (One reason for the choice of site was that part of the Bouzaise flowed through it, providing not only a source of water but a natural means of disposing of all waste material. Beaune five centuries ago was not quite so 'green' as it claims to be today!) If sources are to be believed, Louis XI once remarked of Rolin that since he had caused so much hardship and misery to others during his life it was only fitting that he should have had the hospital built before he died. Records show that quite characteristically Rolin also had his own salvation well in view: '*Dans l'intérêt de mon salut, désirant par un heureux commerce échanger contre les biens célestes, les biens temporels . . . je fonde et dote irrévocablement dans la ville de Beaune un hôpital pour les pauvres malades*' ('In the interest of my own salvation and wanting by a happy stroke of business to exchange worldly possessions for heavenly ones . . . I am establishing and irrevocably giving to the town of Beaune a hospital for the poor sick'). Not even God was spared Rolin's readiness to wheel and deal, and just to remind subsequent generations of his magnanimity his initials are carved everywhere.

The front of the Hôtel-Dieu hardly hints at the splendour inside. A plain, rather severe façade, topped by a grey slate roof, is relieved only by an elaborate porch, a delicate lead frieze along the main ridge and a needle-thin octagonal spire 30 metres high. One particular detail is of note: on the door knocker is a salamander confronting and about to consume a fly. As an animal which survives fire, the former represents justice based on faith; the fly symbolizes disease and death. Beyond the main door you emerge into a beautifully proportioned cobbled courtyard, with a well near the kitchens, and along the south and west sides arcades and a gallery with wooden pillars which give the impression of being a cloister. With the steeply pitched roof, outshot windows, different wood patternings, pinnacles and weather vanes, this is Burgundian Gothic architecture at its best. And there are the tiles. The roofs have all been restored in the twentieth century, but experts are agreed that, as far as it is possible to judge, the colours and intricate arrangements faithfully represent the originals. It is without question one of the finest roofs in Burgundy.

Inside the Hôtel-Dieu the main room is the Grande Salle des Pôvres, 72 metres long and 14 wide. In all, it is a smaller-scale version of the Ancien Hôpital at Tonnerre. As its name suggests, this is where the poorest patients were treated. On each side of the room were fourteen beds (significantly in groups of seven?) with enough room for the patients to observe mass being performed in the chapel behind a screen at the eastern end. They could also admire the great barrel vault of the roof, as well as ponder on the terrors of hell heralded by the heads of fantastic beasts carved in the beam supports. (As light relief there are small heads of people or domestic animals between each pair of these.) This was a place which patients rarely left alive, and where care of the soul was as important as care of the body.

As Beaune's modern hospital has developed during the second half of the twentieth century the Hôtel-Dieu has gone out of business. Once it cared for fifty elderly people, the orphans of Beaune and the poor. But while most of these would be housed in the Salle des Pôvres (sometimes two to a bed), those with financial means could benefit from rather better conditions. The Chambre Sainte-Anne, for example, contained only four beds, and the adjacent Salle Saint-Hugues, added thanks to various gifts made to the foundation in the seventeenth century, was equally reserved for patients who could afford to pay. Given the purpose of the Hôtel-Dieu one remarkable feature of its early years is the absence of a doctor! (Rolin's widow was responsible in 1469 for ensuring that medical visits were at least made on a regular basis.) This should not in any way imply that the first nuns (of whom there were five under a mother superior) were not fully attentive to their patients' needs, and there is evidence of a high degree of hygiene and of care. But, in true medieval fashion, any medical treatment that was administered was aimed at lessening pain rather than at curing its cause. Various syrups and liquids based on herbs and fruit were kept in the *pharmacie* which, in its present form, dates from the eighteenth century, as do the *faïence* pots from Nevers.

No visit to the Hôtel-Dieu is complete without a sight of the polyptych of the Last Judgement by Roger van der Weyden, commissioned by Rolin and listed in the hospital's inventory of 1501. While Christ reigns supreme in the central panel, the real focus of attention is Saint Michael weighing souls and deciding their fate. Along the bottom of the seven lower panels these creatures (whose nudity was considered so shocking in the early nineteenth century that they were clad or hidden by the flames of hell-fire!) go to his right to redemption or left to the abyss of hell. Above them float two groups of supplicating saints, apostles, royalty and churchmen, led by the Virgin and John the Baptist. Saint Michael appears unmoved. Having suffered both from retouching and damp the work was restored in the 1870s; in 1905 it was also split in half so that the paintings on the reverse — formerly visible only when it was shut — could be hung separately. When the restorative work was officially approved in the 1950s by experts in the Louvre, special conditions were recommended for the panels' display. The half million or so visitors who view it every year now do so in a dimly lit room off the Salle Saint-Louis, but there is a large magnifying lens which allows any part of the work to be studied in detail.

If the polyptych and various tapestries represent one form of wealth, the other for which the Hôtel-Dieu and the nearby Hospice de la Charité are noted is wine. On the third Sunday of November in most years since 1859 the world-famous public auction of wine has taken place in the market rooms just opposite the Hôtel-Dieu. Produced from nearly 60 hectares of the most expensive vineyards in Burgundy (nearly all between Aloxe-Corton and Meursault), the wine has been known to reach staggeringly high prices, far outstripping its true worth. Since 1969 it has been issued with the Hospices' own label as a mark of authenticity and quality, but all too frequently the results are disturbingly poor. Despite calls from responsible buyers and tasters across the world for a return to individual estate bottling, the centralized system remains. Certainly the sale is a spectacle. Usually presided over by a well-known public figure, the bids take place while a candle burns; the offer on the table when the candle goes out is successful. Fifty per cent of the takings are donated to the maintenance and improvement of Beaune's medical facilities.

When Stendhal came to Beaune he noted in his travel diaries that he was bored by the inability of the local people to talk about anything other than harvesting grapes. Times have certainly changed, but Beaune remains, for me at least, one of the most private or distant towns in Burgundy. Aware of its position, of its attractions and of its prestige, it makes a superficial appeal to anyone prepared to be won over. But beyond that real contact is difficult. There is, as I suggested earlier, a smugness about the place which may be a form of reaction to the general importance and dominance in the region of Dijon. At the same time it is instructive that, unlike the large majority of Burgundian towns and villages, Beaune does not hold any fair or festival which might be called genuinely popular.

About 7 kilometres directly south of Beaune is a vast tract of forest land stretching eastwards to the valley of the Saône and to its confluence with the Doubs and the Dheune at Verdun. There are few historical landmarks of any note here and what cultivable land there is has mostly been given over to cereal crops and market gardening. But it is a pleasant area to wander through (on bicycle it is easy), following forest paths and watching the fishermen patiently waiting for a fish or maybe an eel to bite which will find its way into the local soup known as *une pochouse*, a kind of fresh-fish *bouillabaisse*, made with white wine and named after the local dialect word for a game bag. The recipe for this varies considerably, but the dish itself is recorded as long ago as the sixteenth century and there is now a Confrérie des Chevaliers de la Pochouse dedicated to keeping the traditions of making it alive.

By contrast, west and south-west of Beaune the limestone ridge continues at around 400 metres. You can climb up quickly to the high point known somewhat presumptuously as the Montagne de Beaune, popular with local people taking family walks and affording a view directly across the motorway north to Savigny-lès-Beaune. More interestingly, the road continues along the ridge to the tiny communities of Bouze and Mavilly-Mandelot and the Gorge du Pas-de-Saint-Martin where you can see the imprint of Saint Martin's horse's hoof as he fled from the devil. Dotted here and there are prehistoric stones, and a few kilometres west, just above La Rochepot by the village of Evelle, are the remains of a medieval settlement. Like the area above Nuits-Saint-Georges, this is spectacular countryside with clumps of thick forest, cut by streams and steep ravines, and is quite unspoiled.

Between Beaune and La Rochepot and the N6 where it joins the N74 at Chagny are yet more of the great Burgundian wine villages: Pommard, Volnay, Meursault and Puligny-Montrachet. The last two produce among the greatest (or best known and most expensive) white wine in the world, made from the Chardonnay grape. Immaculately kept and self-evidently prosperous, these villages have little to offer of historical or artistic interest, though the present Château de Meursault, which dates from the seventeenth century, deserves to be visited. It has been beautifully restored by its present owner, André Boisseaux of the wine conglomerates Patriarche and Kriter, and the land was replanted with vines in the mid 1960s. While the potential profits to be made were no doubt the commanding factor, the purchase of the old vineyards did put an end to a plan to develop a housing estate on them. The first house had in fact already been built; Boisseaux bought it and immediately had it demolished!

Two quite different places in this area should not be missed. The first is the village of La Rochepot, with its château standing on a great spur of rock overlooking the villages of Gamay and Saint-Aubin. Although dating originally from the twelfth century, it was much damaged at the time of the Revolution and fell into general disrepair over the next century. Now restored, with its turrets, pinnacles and coloured roofs rising above the trees, it gives the impression of being a mixture of fortress and fairy-tale castle, especially when glimpsed across the valley from the east. It owes its name to something of a fairy-tale as well. When it was first built the château was called La Roche-Nolay, and in 1403 it was acquired by one Régnier Pot on his return from the Crusades. Legend has it that, having been taken prisoner, he so impressed the sultan Bajazet that he was offered the daughter's hand in marriage. Since he was already married and a Christian he refused, whereupon he was thrown to the lions, but inspired by the Virgin Mary he overcame them and, having once again impressed Bajazet by his bravery, he was released.

Access to the château is by a drawbridge at the rear. There is a walkway (the *chemin de ronde*) from which you look down on the main courtyard. Here is the castle's well, said to be 72 metres deep and to have provided access to a series of underground passages which could be used as escape routes in the event of fire or during attack. While much of the interior reflects the taste of Sadi Carnot, son of the French president between 1887 and 1894, there are features which recall earlier times. The *salle des gardes*, for example, could once have provided refuge for La Rochepot's entire population. In the captain's bedroom above is a statue of the Trinity recovered from the grounds where it had been hidden during the Revolution. The kitchen and the dining room, with its carved and painted ceiling, are not without interest either, but the real delight are the views from a tiny terrace tucked away at the end of the main inner courtyard.

In the middle distance you can see the Archéodrome, just off the A6 in the Aire de Beaune-Tailly. It is easily reached as well from the road which runs from Meursault to Merceuil. While not perhaps the most attractive feature of the landscape, this is the place to take children bored by wine-tastings, archaeological remains and medieval châteaux. In a series of open-air reconstructions, models, dioramas and audio-visual displays indoors you are introduced to Burgundy through the ages. While the emphasis is properly serious and even scholarly, a real attempt has been made to convey to visitors the flavour of life in the distant past. Neolithic huts built from the kinds of material which would have been used 4000 years ago, iron-age burial mounds, a reconstruction of part of the wall built by Caesar's legionaries to prevent Vercingetorix escaping from Alésia, a Roman house and temple, and even a Gallo-Roman garden are just some of the features and exhibits. This is an ongoing project supervised by an international committee and substantially funded by the Société des Autoroutes Paris-Rhin-Rhône.

Just a couple of kilometres after the Archéodrome you leave the *département* of the Côte d'Or and enter that of Saône-et-Loire. The main town of Chalon-sur-Saône on the junction of the river and the Canal du Centre, by way of which it is linked to the Loire at Digoin, is today a wealthy, flourishing commercial centre, marginally bigger than Mâcon and the second town of Burgundy after Dijon. It is still growing and its industrial suburbs – Chalon specializes in photographic and electrical goods, metallurgy, glass ware and kitchen equipment – are hardly attractive. Commercial activity, however, has always been the town's characteristic. But while its position has made it a natural trading centre, it has also resulted in its being the target for numerous attacks from its early history through to the Middle Ages. By the very end of the eighteenth century, with the construction of the canal and fifty years later the creation of the rail link with Paris, Chalon began to enjoy a period of growth and prosperity. Remnants of its medieval trading activities still remain, however, in the form of markets and fairs, especially the two Foires des Sauvagines – the '*foire froide*' on 27 February and the '*foire chaude*' on 25 June. The former specializes in cloth, furs and skins, though since the 1978 law forbidding the sale of squirrel, badger, otter and so on, it attracts far fewer people than it once did; the second is devoted principally to various species of game. There is also a full week's carnival occupying the whole of the town centre at Mardi Gras, when according to tradition local people dress in the most bizarre fashion, floats bear grotesque multicoloured figures made from papier mâché and a competition is held for girls to be named *reine de la Ville*. The carnival at Chalon is generally and with justification considered to be the best in France after the one in Nice.

Gradually Chalon is beginning to realize that it has areas which it can preserve and which attract tourists. The heart and oldest part of the town around the one-time cathedral, Saint-Vincent, now largely a pedestrian area, is not without charm. Many of the houses have fine wrought-iron work, interesting gargoyles, stairways and passages, and there is a hint already here (echoed in Tournus and Mâcon) of the italianate *traboules*, the inner courtyards, galleries and stairs which are found in the older parts of Lyon. The church itself is a mixture and has suffered from vandalism and restoration. Some of the capitals both in the main building and in the cloisters (of Cain and Abel, apocryphal beasts, animals and birds) have been spared, and the neo-Gothic high altar with an early seventeenth-century triptych depicting the crucifixion warrants attention, but there is not a lot more. South from Saint-Vincent, the restored bridge (the original eighteenth-century one was blown up by the Germans in 1944) leads to the little island of Saint-Laurent, now almost entirely occupied by a modern medical complex. What older buildings there were here (and there was a sixteenth-century hospital) have either disappeared altogether or have been incorporated in the modern ones, though some, such as part of the kitchens, can be visited on request. But the main reason for coming to the island is for the fine view you have of the river frontage on the north side and particularly of the Quais des Messageries and de la Poterne, which were once the hub of Chalon's fishing activities. Just near by in the Place Sainte-Marie a new Maison de l'Environnement is being built, funded jointly by town, region and national government; it is yet another sign of Burgundy's concern for its natural heritage.

From the island you can also see what is perhaps the best known of Chalon's buildings, the Musée Nicéphore Niepce in the elegant Hôtel des Messageries Royales. This is a tribute to the man who discovered the principle of photography in 1816 using a spectacle lens and a box. The work and discoveries of other key photographers – Daguerre and Fox Talbot, for example – are displayed here as well as pieces of equipment used or photographs taken by more modern figures such as the famous portraitist Nadar or Robert Doisneau. This is a serious, technical museum, but for anyone interested in the evolution and art of photography it is a fascinating and rewarding place in which to spend time. It alone makes Chalon worth visiting.

To the south of Chalon lies the beginning of the Mâconnais region. To the north-west, in a triangle bounded on the sides by the Canal du Centre with Chagny at its most northern point and by the N80 running along its base, is a most attractive area criss-crossed by narrow, steep roads and by numerous streams and small rivers – the Thalie, Orbise and Verrière – running down from the central spine of hills which reach their high point near Châtel-Moron at nearly 500 metres. The centre of this region is known as La Vallée des Vaux (literally, valley of the valleys) and it all repays a leisurely visit. Rully, Mercurey and Givry, if not as prestigious as some of their relatively near neighbours, produce delightful wines, often at much more reasonable prices; and in smaller villages, where production is so small there is no point in the *viticulteur*'s trying to become commercial on any scale, there are real bargains to be found. There are interesting places to see and visit as well: Chamilly, with its church spire in the shape of an obelisk and with a stone in the surround of the south door which harvesters for centuries have used for sharpening their scythes; Marloux, where an effigy of the Virgin Mary has until quite recently been held locally to cure sick children and even bring still-born ones to life; Châtel-Moron, where the church has some stone tubs ornamented with crudely carved heads and said to be Roman in origin; Germolles, whose château, once owned by the dukes of Burgundy, has rare heraldic frescos; the massive fortified medieval farm on the edge of Saint Mard-de-Vaux; the château (visits inside are by appointment only) just south of Rully which has belonged to the Montesus family for nearly 400 years; or the grottos of Agneux. All this and more, but wine wins in the end. At the end of a day's sightseeing few places are more agreeable to relax in and sample a glass of white Burgundy from nearby Rully than the vast shady square at Saint-Jean-de-Vaux.

4
The Pull of the Midi

The southernmost part of modern Burgundy is arguably the most varied but curiously neglected of the whole region. With the exception of Tournus and Mâcon, of the abbey at Cluny, of the great prehistoric site at Solutré or the wine villages of Pouilly and Fuissé, this is an area often bypassed by tourists as they hurtle by train or car towards Lyon and beyond to the attractions of Provence and the Mediterranean coast. The loss is theirs, for this part of the *département* of Saône-et-Loire, much of which is generally known as the Mâconnais, offers a multitude of delights for anyone with the patience and time to explore and seek them out.

The differences from the Côte d'Or are many and travellers have frequently commented on how already by Tournus, just 20 kilometres south of Chalon, the influence of the Midi can be felt. 'There are fewer differences between Tournus and Avignon', wrote Joseph Bard 150 years ago, 'than there are between Tournus and Chalon'. Everything changes, he said – habits, traditions, atmosphere, methods of farming, architecture, and so on. An examination of almost any cluster of village roofs quickly illustrates this point today. The pitch is less steep, and the flat tiles of northern and central Burgundy are gradually replaced by the interlocking rounded ones known in the south as *tuiles romaines*. And language too begins to change. Dialect words tend now to be those of the south, influenced by Latin. The word for a traditional farmhouse south of Tournus, for example, is usually the Provençal *mas*; just to the north it is likely to be *meix*.

This whole region is crossed by a series of valleys and ridges running north–south. To the extreme east is the Saône which, after looping away from the main N6 just south of Chalon, rejoins it at Tournus and flows more or less alongside the road to Mâcon. This remains one of the most attractive stretches of any major river in France. Large areas of the banks are still covered with rushes and wild irises and the river has great carpets of water-lilies. But few signs of past life remain. Local people still fish here from their long, shallow-bottomed boats but they are subject to strict controls and regulations. Large nets are no longer allowed, though small ones known as *carrelets* and suspended like baskets from a pulley are still used, as are hand-held nets (*éperviers*) and lines, each one of which may have up to eighteen hooks. Local people claim that the Saône has over thirty varieties of fish with carp, tench and catfish being amongst the most common. Pike too are found, but such has been the demand during the last decade or so that the river has to be regularly restocked. Just over fifty years ago too the traditional method of duck-shooting was still allowed. This was carried out from a boat (*arlequin*), about 4 metres long and sitting low in the water. A single gunshot would be fired to raise the ducks, who would then be indiscriminately blasted by pellets from the *canardière* as they flew up. A successful (and profitable) day's shooting could produce fifty or more *pièces*, but many ducks would be wounded and left to die. Duck-shooting is now officially permitted only from hides built along the Saône's banks.

Old photographs and descriptions of life along this stretch of the river reveal thriving and busy communities and other activities. In addition to those who earned their living from fishing and duck-shooting were the professional washerwomen, for example, who scrubbed clothes collected from the local villages in wheelbarrows. The more fortunate ones worked inside boats specially built for this purpose, but others, particularly in the smaller communities, were obliged to work outside on the river bank all the year round and in all weathers. Towing by horses was normal until the 1920s and, before any locks had been built, pine and oak logs were moved down river to Lyon and beyond to Arles and Beaucaire in the form of huge rafts. These could be 100 metres in length, the large trunks strapped together by saplings and the branches of younger trees. The *radeleurs*, as they were known, lived on their rafts either in tents or in primitive wooden shacks. The journey could be precarious. With the exception of fishing, most if not all of these local activities have disappeared from the Saône by the late twentieth century. In their place have emerged power-driven commercial traffic, pleasure launches, barges and speedboats. The link with the Loire by way of the Canal du Centre has largely contributed to this and when or if the link is eventually made with the Rhine there will almost inevitably be a dramatic rise in pollution. At present this is not a particular problem but the regular and often boisterous disturbance of the water causes damage to the banks and hence to the habitat of wildlife, dredging affects that of different species of fish and the general attempt to 'tidy up' sections of the river has altered the natural currents and in places has resulted in stagnation. Even so, especially on an early morning in autumn or in February, as the mists swirl across the surface of the Saône it is easy to forget the presence of the late twentieth century in the form of the nearby motorway or railway line and slip back into a timeless past.

Immediately to the west, across the A6 and just to the south of Chalon, are the extensive forests of Givry and La Ferté, spotted with *étangs* and marshy areas; thereafter is the first of the lines of hills about 40 kilometres long which run south from Sennecey to Pouilly and Fuissé. The east-facing slopes of these are substantially given over to the cultivation of the vine and several of the villages, notably Viré and Clessé north of Mâcon and Saint-Vérand, Pouilly, Fuissé and Loche to the west and south provide some of the best Mâconnais white wines. While it has to be acknowledged that they may not rival those of Meursault or the Montrachets, at their best they are full of charm and flavour and certainly much cheaper. (A little red wine is made, some of it good, but white from the Chardonnay grape dominates.) Just as the monks at Cîteaux were responsible for the cultivation of the vineyards at Vougeot, so their counterparts at Cluny and Tournus were for those here. During the late Middle Ages local customs barriers, taxes and rivalries made the exportation of wine beyond the region difficult, and when it was attempted the rivers would often be too low in summer or ice-bound in winter. According to one local story, the breakthrough was achieved in the eighteenth century when a *vigneron*, Claude Brosse, decided to take some samples of his wine to the king at Versailles. This he did by cart, the journey lasting thirty-three days. He was noticed by Louis XIV who tasted Brosse's wine and found it to his liking whereupon it was sycophantically adopted by the court. The reputation of the Mâconnais Blanc was made.

Just to the south of Mâcon is the Beaujolais, an area of tightly packed hills with roads twisting in and out of a patchwork of vines. With the exception of the Pouilly-Fuissé area there is more space around Viré and Clessé. The *route des vins* is accurately so called, but because of the uncertainty of the climate the importance of a vineyard's site here is even greater than in the Côte d'Or. The result of this is that the vineyards are broken up by orchards, clumps of woodland, meadows and fields of sunflowers creating a varied and attractive landscape. Vines are also grown differently. While two fruit-bearing shoots are carefully trained along their supporting wires, the plant is often allowed to grow higher than is traditional elsewhere in the area – a method which means that fewer vines (and hence less labour) per hectare are required. But it also means that the top bunches of grapes do not benefit fully from the heat reflected off the ground or stored in the stones around the vine's stem, with the consequent risk of increased acidity in the wine. Experimentation, whether in growing techniques, in treatment or, ultimately, in vinification is the norm, and many growers have too small an area for them to be able to risk remaining independent. The result is that they sell their grapes to one of the *caves co-opératives* of the region (of which there are now more than twenty) which generally produce excellent wine at very competitive prices. All that is to be hoped is that, while it has undoubtedly benefited from an aggressive marketing campaign over the last few years, Mâconnais Blanc does not find itself in the position of Beaujolais where artificially created demand has too often resulted in indifferent and overpriced wine.

The line of hills where the vines are cultivated rises to between 350 and 450 metres and is crossed by three small rivers which flow down into the Saône, the Bourbonne, the Monge and the Petite Grosne. Beyond, just a few kilometres further west, the countryside begins to change. The vine still remains prominent and there are important *caves co-opératives* in villages such as Lugny, but increasingly the new slopes are wooded with oaks, beech, chestnut, maples and conifers. There are a number of roads cutting across the hills here, providing some dramatic views, notably at the Col des Chèvres, the Col de Brancion and the Col de la Pistole. But it is infinitely more interesting to begin at Sermaizey (while not failing to visit the newly restored eleventh-century church of Saint-Martin, with its stone-covered roof), cross to Sennecey and thereafter follow the narrow, twisting road through Montceaux-Ragny south towards Brancion. For those so inclined it is also possible to pick up the Grande Randonnée 76A in Sermaizey and continue along the crest of the hills in the same direction to end in either Cluny or in Berzé. This amounts to a walk of just over 40 kilometres, but one which is not difficult and which passes through enough communities for refreshment or even a night's accommodation to be easily found. The first major point of call is Brancion itself, but a number of places merit attention even if they are not always open to the public. The first of these is the beautifully maintained Château de la Tour de Sennecey at Ruffey, with its three round towers and keep-like central house set back among the trees of a vast estate. Just after Montreaux-Ragny – the smallest *commune* in the whole of Saône-et-Loire with barely two dozen inhabitants – the road forks at Corlay. By taking either direction it is possible to skirt round an attractive area of woodland (Bois de Mancey) and vines by way of Étrigny or Mancey. The Grande Randonnée 76A also provides easy access on foot and allows you to visit the Roche d'Aujoux, almost the highest point at 483 metres and from which there is a view west over the valley of the Grosne. At its foot in the village of Balleure are some elegant eighteenth-century fountains which appear rather incongruous in this deeply rural spot, but it is the château and its legend which really attract. A local story tells how a one-time lord of Balleure was attending Christmas Eve mass in the local church when he heard his favourite dog Garelaut barking. Being first and foremost a hunter he immediately forgot his Christian obligations and went off to find his dog, which had succeeded in raising a huge stag. The lord hunted it throughout the night and the following day before finding himself at dusk on the Roche d'Aujoux. The stag jumped from the high point to safety; Balleure tried to follow and fell to his death. His body and presumably his soul were collected by the Devil himself, who then marked the ground with his hoof before disappearing with a great roar of laughter. A local superstition has it that on certain nights Garelaut's barking and his master's call can still be heard – a chill warning to all those who feel inclined to turn away from their faith.

Having rejoined the D182 you navigate your way through Dulphey with its long winemaker's house and thereafter the cluster of tiny stone dwellings and narrow streets which forms Royer and climb up to Brancion high on its spur of rock and enjoying views towards both the Saône and the Grosne. Originally a Gallo-Roman encampment called Brancedunum, it had become by the early Middle Ages the seat of the lords of Brancion, who were the biggest landowners in the area. The lords ruined themselves financially during the Crusades and were obliged to sell the château which subsequently passed through various hands. It has been much restored, first in the sixteenth century and more recently since the 1860s when it was bought by the family from which the present owners are directly descended. Now it is one of the most impressive official *monuments historiques* in the region, with enough reconstructed features (kitchen, lavatories, defences, for example) to enable visitors to Brancion to conjure up a good picture of castle life in the Middle Ages. It also becomes quickly apparent how impregnable the château was; in fact it is said to have fallen on a single occasion in 1584 during the Wars of Religion and only then because of treachery.

Down from the castle the village itself contains several gems – the covered fifteenth-century market place and a number of smartly restored houses a century or more older which are now in heavy demand as *résidences secondaires* (as the number-plates of parked cars will instantly suggest). The charm of this is self-evident, especially in spring or summer, but Brancion under snow or whipped by a north-easterly wind is entirely another matter, and such conditions serve once again to remind us that medieval living was all too frequently far from comfortable. Finally the tiny, dumpy twelfth-century church of Saint-Pierre on the opposite side of the promontory from the château has to be visited. Although experts claim that the church was built in two different periods, there is a feeling of unity and simplicity here which is absolutely typical of the best of Burgundy's Romanesque churches. At one time it would have been decorated, of course, and fragments of thirteenth-century frescos are visible. One, which depicts the infant Jesus tightly wrapped in swaddling clothes and lying on a shelf in a kind of wall cupboard while his mother rests, is a pleasant and very human relief from some of the more usual formal representations of Christ's early infancy. At the head of the north aisle is the effigy of Jocerand de Brancion, who was killed at Mansourah where he was fighting with Louis XI on the Sixth Crusade. Other funerary slabs, dating from the seventeenth and eighteenth centuries, bear the names of local notables from Brancion and nearby Martailly.

Before exploring even further into the heart of this northernmost corner of the Mâconnais, Tournus remains to be visited. On the way from Brancion the road follows the contours of the hill alongside the valley of the Natouze to the village of Ozenay. Right down by the river stands the château, now part of a privately owned farm, and which, though said to have been built in the sixteenth and seventeenth centuries, appears considerably older. The roof is completely covered in the local stone tiles (*laves*) and inside are several horseshoe-shaped fireplaces called *sarrasines* which are virtually unknown on the west side of the Saône. Also to be found in a small bedroom next to the *salle des gardes* are wooden panels painted with scenes from the fables written in the seventeenth century by La Fontaine. The château is not normally open to the public but the present owners are not unwilling to allow anyone who shows genuine interest to see these features. But neither they nor any of the historical or archaeological books on the area I have consulted can offer an explanation of this curious assortment; it is as though a member of the Barthelot family, in whose possession the château was for 300 years, either decided to be self-indulgent or was genuinely interested in bringing into what was otherwise a somewhat austere building touches of culture or architectural features which he (or she) had seen elsewhere and found attractive.

Tournus

Perched along the edge of the Saône and backed by the hills of the eastern edge of the Mâconnais, Tournus is a delightful town. As we have already noted it is generally recognized as marking a point where the influence of the Midi begins to become apparent and certainly in atmosphere alone there is a liveliness and bustle about the place which you would more normally associate with, say, Avignon or Arles. While Tournus was never a major crossing place like its northern neighbour Chalon, it was a trading point for the salt merchants who came from Lons-le-Saulnier to the east and, more importantly, developed as a staging and supply post for the Romans on the Via Agrippa in the first century. The Romans called it Castrum Trenorchium, and traces of their presence can still be found in some of the cellars of houses in the southern area of the present town around the church of Sainte-Madeleine. But it was not until the sixth century and the establishment of Christianity that Tournus began to emerge with its own significance and identity. Already in 179 an early Christian, Valerian, had been beheaded by the Romans and a cult began to develop around his memory. According to Gregory of Tours a small abbey existed in Tournus in the sixth century, possibly authorized by the Frankish king Gontran. Three hundred years later, in 875, some monks arrived from the west coast of France bearing with them the relics of their own patron saint, Philibert, who had died in 685. Persecuted by the Normans, they had been forced to leave their abbey at Noirmoutier and, according to popular histories, had set out on a journey which was going to take forty years! As they crossed France miraculous healings were witnessed and on their arrival at Tournus such was the prestige of Philibert that Valerian was pushed into second place. Not surprisingly, this caused some friction, and in the middle of the tenth century a series of disputes forced the 'newcomers' to leave for the Auvergne. After three years such were the misfortunes (famine, miscarriages, bad weather) to befall Tournus that a special delegation was sent begging them to return. This they agreed to do, and the fact that the abbey church is known today as Saint-Philibert indicates clearly enough where the real power and prestige would lie. Thereafter the abbey grew increasingly influential and remained independent of Cluny. Relations between the monks and ordinary citizens were not always harmonious as the former levied taxes and made various demands on the *tournusiens*, including the right to obtain the family bed on the death of a house owner so as to ensure that the abbey's guest rooms were always well furnished. Nevertheless the activities of the abbey did form the basis for Tournus' prestige and wealth throughout the Middle Ages. During this period winemaking, fishing, curing, farming and quarrying all flourished and continued to do so until the last years of the nineteenth century. Since then some light industries have developed — notably for household goods — but most of all Tournus relies for its income on those modern pilgrims, the tourists who flock here every year in their tens of thousands and on many days swell the local population of 7500 by more than 100 per cent.

Situated at the northern point of the town, Saint-Philibert was once completely surrounded and protected by walls with nine towers. An impression of fortification still remains if you approach the main door of the church through the narrow gateway along the Rue Thibaudet, and were it not for its belfry and spire (added in the late twelfth century) even the west façade, rising massively to over 30 metres with its seven long narrow windows like arrow slits, would seem more suited to a military castle than to a church. Beyond the door is the narthex. On the ground floor the four heavy pillars ($1\frac{1}{2}$ metres in diameter) give you an instant sense of the mass not just of the chapel above but of the church as a whole. One curious feature of this entrance are several round engraved slabs, dating from the sixteenth century, which are thought to cover tombs dug in the form of wells. Above in Saint Michael's chapel are some examples of very early Romanesque carving: note in particular the head of a man with staring eyes and splayed ears as well as the figure of a workman holding a mallet in his left hand and giving a blessing with his right. Once it was possible to go from this chapel directly into the main nave but since the seventeenth century the way has been blocked by the organ. Now from the ground floor the impact is immediate.

While we can still see quite clearly the same basic bare style our attention is drawn upwards to the roof, a series of five barrel vaults crossing from the lateral bays, separated by double arches with alternate pink and white stones which suggest the influence of Moorish architecture and echo on a less grand scale the same decorative feature to be found in the Basilique Sainte-Madeleine at Vézelay. Four chapels give off the main nave, all decorated at a later date, but only one is of note and this on account of the cedarwood reliquary in the form of a statue of Mary with a remarkably adult Christ sitting on her knee. Known as 'Notre Dame la Brune' it dates from the twelfth century and, so experts tell us, originates from the Auvergne. Mary's hands and head are disproportionately large and rather disturb the general balance of the statue, but the sculptor has succeeded in capturing the serenity of her gaze.

Beyond the nave the crossing, choir and ambulatory, which at ground floor level have been much restored, appear fussy and rather cramped. However, some of the carving of animals and plants around the higher windows and on the capitals is original. Beneath lies the crypt, dedicated to Valerian, which has suffered far less at the hands of the restorers and with its poor lighting is probably very much as it was nearly 1000 years ago. Directly beneath the altar is a tomb, by tradition that of Valerian. The relics of Philibert, superior even in this, lie above in an ornate, glass-fronted chest in a chapel off the choir.

Outside the main body of the church are the other abbey buildings, including the cloisters, though only the gallery alongside the south wall of the church is original. The most interesting of these buildings is the former refectory, 30 metres long and known locally as 'le Ballon' in memory of the various ball games (especially *jeu de paume*) which the monks are said to have played here. It is certainly one of the finest examples of a Romanesque refectory in France and both it and the adjoining rooms are used regularly and most successfully for exhibitions and for concerts throughout the year.

South and east of Saint-Philibert and down to the river are several streets whose names recall important medieval trades and occupations: Rue du Grenier à Sel (salt), Rue des Saules (basket work), Rue des Tonneliers (wine), Rue des Bateliers (river transport) or Rue de la Poissonnerie (fish). Just below the roofs of the houses in the last of these you will see lugs made of stone or wood and with a hole in their centre. These were used to support long rods from which fishing nets or animal hides were hung to dry. Another area bearing traces of its medieval past is centred on the Rue du Bief Potet. Here the tall, wood-strapped houses once inhabited by leather workers are being purchased as second homes by French and foreigners alike, and the bright interiors and modern kitchen equipment are a far cry from the dingy and insalubrious conditions of the fourteenth or fifteenth centuries. Near by in the Rue de l'Hôpital is a house where mass was defiantly celebrated in secret during the Revolution, and immediately adjacent is the seventeenth-century Hôtel-Dieu. This has now been shut for several years while restoration work is carried out, but it is reputed to be as impressive inside as the Hôtel-Dieu in Beaune, and from prints and photographs clearly possesses a fine and important *pharmacie*. The church itself was built in the twelfth century, almost certainly on the site of a Roman temple. Much damaged during the Revolution when it was reduced to being a wine store, it was not properly restored until the 1970s. While little remains of any note, some of the carving is good and there is some especially fine – and original – stone lacework on the columns around the main door. But the immediate surroundings are full of attractions. Nearly all of the streets here were developed between the fifteenth and seventeenth centuries and these are splendid examples of houses with arcades, galleries and balconies, reminders of former prosperity and pride. There is also a curious feature. Between the bridge and the church of Sainte-Madeleine, a stretch of about 500 metres, there is no street which provides easy access to the riverside. There are, however, various interlinking passages – anticipating the *traboules* to be found in Mâcon and Lyon – which give this lower section of Tournus a special feeling of intimacy and even mystery. The best time to visit it is on a Saturday, the day of the regular street market. And no visit to the town is complete without making a short excursion across the river, not only for a fine view of the town with the Romanesque towers of Saint-Philibert rising above the roofs, but to explore the villages of

Lacrost and Préty whose quarries over the centuries have provided the pink limestone for so much of the local building.

Even if legend has exaggerated the length of time it took the monks to cross France from Noirmoutier, any visit their successors might have paid to their colleagues in Cluny four or five hundred years ago would certainly have taken two or three days and would not have been without risk from roaming bands of brigands. For the modern traveller the journey is both quicker and safer. He has two basic options, either west through Brancion or south alongside the Saône and then west by way of Viré and Azé.

By the more northern of these the road wanders down after Brancion through thick woods, crosses the pretty valleys of the Grison and the Bisançon and almost without warning arrives at a junction with four others (originally forest tracks) in the village of Chapaize. The handful of houses are dominated by the church of Saint-Martin, originally part of a Benedictine priory founded by monks from Chalon early in the eleventh century, and another of the many Romanesque delights to be discovered in the Mâconnais. The similarities with Saint-Philibert are obvious, and while it is easy to see where modification and restoration have been carried out, the essentials of the original church remain clear. Especially impressive are the massive, squat pillars above which are the arches of a slightly later roof after the first had collapsed, and the tower which at 35 metres seems disproportionately high. The outside stairway to the base of this is a reminder, however, that this was also a look-out point and that, while not as heavily fortified as some Provençal churches, Saint-Martin would have served in need as a place of refuge. On the other side, high up and looking north, is the carved figure of a man with large splayed ears and with his hands clasped over his private parts, known as the man 'who sees and hears everything'. Just next door to the church is a house owned by a lady who sells a variety of artisanal products and bunches of herbs. Over the years she has kept a sharp eye on the restorative work that has been going on and is both knowledgeable and critical. She once interrupted cutting back her irises to give me a lesson on the lack of thought in the retention of the opening of what (she said) was clearly a nineteenth-century window in the west wall. Not only did it allow in more light than the original medieval one would have done, it upset the balance of the whole façade. She also deplored the use of machined planks of wood for the remaking of the main door. This meant that the irregular pattern created by the different sizes of planks as they were cut from a single trunk was lost. In both cases I could not help feeling that she had a point.

Little remains of the former priory, though the buildings, now forming a most elegant private house on the north side of the church, the well and gardens are obviously in large part original. On the western edge of the village as well is a neat, round tower with arrow slits which probably formed part of the priory's outside walls.

From Chapaize the road continues directly to Cormatin, but every attempt should be made to visit Lancharre just to the north-east of the village, less for the remains of its Romanesque church than for its delightful village square with its well, *lavoir* and trim traditional houses. And from here, equally worthwhile is Sercy, if only to admire its curious and remarkable château set back from the road across lawns, box hedges and a small lake. The château was begun in the twelfth century, and remained the property of the same family for 700 years. Powerful and influential, the Sercy household was not without rivals and the care with which the château was fortified can still be seen, despite serious damage by fire in 1929. While permitted by appointment, visits are not encouraged, but the five irregular towers and almost unique style of intricate, open woodwork in the roof on the Tour du Hourd can be admired from a distance.

The power and authority symbolized by a fortified château like Sercy are replaced within 10 kilometres by the seventeenth-century elegance of Cormatin. (The two châteaux were once briefly owned by the same family in the late eighteenth century.) When it was first built, the inner courtyard was hidden from view by a wall which rose above the first floor. Fortunately this was demolished at the end of the century, as was the southern wing which after the Revolution had been turned into a calico printing factory by an industrialist from Lyon. The outside of the château is therefore much more spacious and open than it once was, and this contributes to its present elegance, enhanced too by the magnificent restoration of the grounds (including a new maze) and the moat – once one of the symbols of aristocratic status. Inside, the monumental staircase with its pink, white and pale golden stonework is most elegant as are the restored suites of rooms with their ornately decorated, beamed ceilings. We are reminded too of the symbolism of colours here. The lord's bedroom is in red-brown, signifying authority; his wife's is in blue for faithfulness. The kitchens, domestic rooms and cellars have also been refurbished, but even modern techniques cannot prevent their being almost permanently damp, so high is the water-table in this region – a reminder that, for all the elegance on the floors above, a servant's lot was far from being comfortable.

In the course of its history Cormatin has had some illustrious visitors and occupants. Probably most famous of all was Lamartine, who had an affair with the owner's daughter, Nina de Pierreclau, and whose romantic, reflective wanderings are remembered in the 400-metre-long walk borded by lime trees known as the *allée de Lamartine*. The singer Caruso was a visitor, as was the French composer Massenet, and in 1888 the novelist Jacques de Lacretelle (who owes his fame above all to *Silbermann* (1922)) was born here. Today's visitors are tourists who find Cormatin an ideal stopping place between Chalon and Cluny. The château is fortunate, of course, since the money from their entrance fees together with income from musical and theatrical activities during the summer months goes towards the cost of restoration. But this is another outstanding example of French government policy towards important historic buildings. While the present owners have to provide 25 per cent of the money required, the state contributes 50 per cent and Saône-et-Loire the rest.

Only 4 kilometres south from Cormatin is Taizé, the centre of an important ecumenical movement. The idea was conceived in 1940 by a young Swiss pastor, Roger Schutz, who was visiting Cluny from Lausanne. He bought a house in the village and by 1944 he and six fellow priests had established their community. Visitors to Taizé should not expect a modern abbey. Instead tents, chalets and car-parks suggest more a holiday camp than a spiritual retreat, and the airy modern (1962) Église de la Réconciliation with its bare concrete walls, banked seating and modern stained-glass windows presents a stark contrast to the tiny and equally bare Romanesque church on the opposite side of the village. For much of the year Taizé is quiet but at Easter in particular it attracts thousands of young people who submit themselves for a week to the discipline of monastery life. There are those who regard the Taizé experiment with a degree of scepticism, but the community has retained its appeal and has established international links, especially with third-world countries. Moreover, at a time when reconciliation seems to be increasingly difficult and religious fundamentalism is growing, Taizé provides a unique glimpse of what might be achieved.

To reach Cluny by the lower route, the most attractive way is to leave the main road and the river at Fleurville and after Viré make a loop round just north of the village to take in the view from Burgy. (The road is indicated as '*Burgy par la montagne Belvédère*'.) Then by way of Péronne you arrive at Azé where there is the most extensive cave system in Burgundy and one of France's most important archeological sites. An underground river flows through one of the two principal caves open to the public, and there is an impressive array of stalactites and stalagmites. Excavations have produced evidence to show that first animals and later man have lived in these caves for nearly half a million years. The bones of rhinoceros, elephants, lions and bears have been found as well as those of prehistoric man, together with various kinds of primitive flint tools and weapons. These and many other discoveries from the region can be seen in a small museum at the entrance. The water which flows underground here has its sources, it is generally agreed, in the granite hills just to the north, covered by the forest of Goulaine and reaching nearly 600 metres at the Montagne Saint-Romain. The system is not nearly as big as some in the Ardèche or as that feeding the Fontaine de Vaucluse in Provence, nor, as far as I know, has it produced any popular legends, but it is an interesting, worthwhile and yet another different feature of this fascinating corner of the Mâconnais.

From Azé the road climbs steeply up to the aptly named Col des Quatre Vents before winding down through forests and gentler slopes to the valley of the Grosne. Opposite lies Cluny, which, despite periods of destruction and dispute, still permits us to imagine what one of the most harmonious and complete set of religious, civil and military buildings certainly in all of Burgundy, if not Europe as a whole, must have been like.

Cluny

Watered by the Grosne and protected to the west by hills, Cluny's site was appreciated by early tribal settlements and subsequently by the Romans who gave it the name of Cluniacum. By the Middle Ages the town had grown to its present size and, like Tournus, depended almost entirely on the abbey for its wealth and prestige. Its foundation dates from 910 and the first church from 927. Twelve monks of the order of Saint Benedict accompanied the first abbot, Bernon, but such was the rate of growth that within two centuries that number had risen to 300. During this period too the size of the church was increased and records suggest that Cluny II, as it is known (completed in 1010), was comparable to Saint-Philibert in Tournus. The design of Chapaize today is thought to resemble it. But, as is so well known, expansion (and ambition) did not stop there. Throughout the rest of France, and indeed Europe and the Holy Lands, over 1000 Cluniac monasteries or dependent institutions were set up, forming an impressive and powerful spiritual empire. By the late eleventh century the home church was expanded further and before Saint Peter's was built in Rome Cluny III, completed by 1130, was the biggest church in Christendom: 187 metres long, 41 metres wide, 30 metres high and with its towers rising 20 metres higher. It served as a model for various Late Romanesque churches thereafter, notably those at Paray-le-Monial and at La Charité-sur-Loire. Such was Cluny's influence that the abbots succeeded in creating special links with Rome which effectively gave them independence of all but the Pope. Gradually, as the power and wealth of the community grew, so the spiritual order began to be less than rigorously observed and Bernard was asked to intervene. But to no avail. Cluny was materially wealthy and became a target for attack. The wars of religion brought damage, the magnificent library was pillaged by the Huguenots, the Revolution added to the misery and by the early nineteenth century what was left of the buildings was sold to an entrepreneur from Mâcon, one Batonard, who used them for building material.

What had once been what the literary critic Albert Thibaudet imagined as '*un Versailles bénédictin*' had become a builders' yard.

Any visit paid to Cluny today requires therefore a good deal of imagination, but it can be helped by the models which have been built, thanks largely to the work of the American archeologist from the University of Harvard, the late Kenneth Conant. These can be seen in the Musée Ochier, named after a nineteenth-century doctor who was amongst the first to begin to preserve what he could find of Cluny's past. This museum, which has only recently been reorganized, also contains some capitals which were once in the abbey choir and which depict local medieval activities – such as music-making and bee-keeping – as well as standard religious motifs and floral patterns. The museum is at the entrance to gardens (in the fourteenth century an orchard) north of the abbey where the town hall now is. This was once the residence of Jacques d'Amboise, begun around 1500 but much modified subsequently and now a rather unhappy mix of 300 years of architectural styles. Just next to these gardens across the Rue Porte des Prés is a stud farm, the Haras National, one of only five in France. It was created by Napoleon in 1806 and today is responsible for the siring of all kinds of horses, from pure-bred race-horses to working animals for farms. Many of the original stable buildings are of stone taken from the abbey ruins.

A fine view over the town and, if you have a plan, an idea of how Cluny was laid out six hundred years ago, can be had by climbing the 120 wooden steps of the Tour des Fromages where the tourist office now is. But more rewarding in my view is to stroll through the streets, ideally on a late autumn afternoon when the colours mellow and the tourists have gone, and examine at leisure the range of ordinary citizens' houses from the twelfth to the fourteenth centuries. These are grouped mainly in the area on the west side of the town comprising principally the Rue de la République and the Rue d'Avril. The large central entrance of these houses would have originally given access to a ground floor cellar or a small shop and the staircase leading to the living accommodation above would be by the adjacent door. Internal access only became the norm from the thirteenth century. The first floor windows in several of these houses are in a series of neat Romanesque arches separated by slender pillars with carved capitals – a sign not only of secular prosperity but of the abbey's influence here as well.

If to the east the edge of the Mâconnais is signalled by the Saône, to the west no such clear indicator is to be found, though the valley of the Grosne is convenient. Thereafter the land continues to rise gently, drops slightly by the valley of the Bourbince and the Canal du Centre, and begins to rise again, especially towards the north-west and the foothills of the Morvan. The southern boundary is equally unclear as the hills of the Beaujolais announce themselves, but from Mâcon it may be considered to run approximately just south of the route taken by the N79 through Brandon and Charolles dipping to encompass Fuissé, Pouilly and Milly-Lamartine. Certainly people who live just to the south in villages such as Tramayes, Matour or La Clayette are of the clear opinion that Burgundy lies to the north. The departmental boundaries here, as in the north-west corner of Burgundy, may be helpful but not absolute. What is certain is that Mâcon can legitimately be considered to mark the furthest south-eastern point of both the Mâconnais and of Burgundy as a whole.

Mâcon

The strategic importance of Mâcon's site – a meeting place of Burgundy, Beaujolais and the Bresse across the Saône – has been recognized by man from earliest times, as excavations in the area have revealed. It seems that around 300 BC a fortified camp known as Matisco was established by the Aedui (just to the north of the present town centre), which the Romans then subsequently developed, transforming it into a major stopping place on the Via Agrippa. Mâcon suffered from attacks by Germanic tribes from the east and throughout the Middle Ages from much local feuding. In more recent years it has resisted the spreading administrative importance of Dijon, and the more immediate challenge – in terms of business and tourism – of Chalon, which is twice its size. It is safe to say, however, that by and large Mâcon appears to have won. The construction of the canal has meant that while the town continues to benefit from trade brought by water, the medieval bridge, the much repaired Pont Saint-Laurent, has been preserved and acts as a focal point for thousands of tourists, as it provides the best view of the long sweep of the town's eastern façade, fringed by the Quai Lamartine with its immaculately tended gardens and lawns. In the twentieth century, and especially during the last fifty years, Mâcon has expanded rapidly. Its population has doubled (there is an important and well-integrated Portuguese community here), light industry has developed (copper piping, motors, printing, match-making and illustrated postcards) and the proximity of the A6 and the creation of a TGV station at nearby Loché are all important factors. In May one of France's greatest wine festivals is held at the Parc des Expositions, just on the north side of town near the new theatre and cultural centre – a fitting tribute to Saint Vincent, patron saint of winemakers, whose relics were brought to Mâcon from Spain in 543 by the Frankish king Childebert.

Central Mâcon is easily explored on foot within a day. From the Pont Saint-Laurent the Rue de la Barre divides the town conveniently in two. To the south is the town hall, originally the private house of the Comte de Montrevel, a rich landowner from the Bresse. Despite his genuine sympathy for the Revolution, Montrevel refused to abandon his lands and wealth and emigrate; in February 1794 he was arrested and five months later beheaded. Many of the original features of his house have been lost, but parts of the kitchens remain, including the massive fireplace, and a sumptuous stone stairway with rich wrought-iron balustrades which climbs through the three storeys. Behind the town hall lies the heavy and impersonal church of Saint-Pierre, and just to the south the restored eighteenth-century Hospice de la Charité. The latter, now a home for elderly people, has one of the rare examples of a '*tour des enfants abandonnés*'. This is a revolving door rather like a barrel through which abandoned, new-born babies could be put by their unfortunate mothers who, having alerted the guardian, could slip away unseen.

This group of buildings is overseen by Alexandre Falguière's statue of Lamartine who, with his cloak draped romantically about him, resolutely stares in the direction of Paris where he hoped ambition would be rewarded and fame secured. The museum devoted to his life and exploits, but housing a general collection as well, is directly north in the Rue Sigorgne. Just near by in the Rue Carnot is the Maison de Bois, a sixteenth-century house believed to have been initially the meeting place of a drinking society and known as the Abbaye de Maugouvert. (A *maugouvert* was someone who behaved badly or riotously, literally who 'governed himself badly'.) Some of the carvings on the first and second floors are mildly licentious (a gorilla with an erection, for example) or amusing (drunken griffins). The house is now a café, complete with juke-box and pinball-tables.

The northern side of Mâcon, beyond the Rue de la Barre, contains the remains of the old Romanesque cathedral of Saint-Vincent. On display in the narthex and two towers are pieces of sculpture and archeological finds, and a cabinet in which a series of prints illustrate how, until its demolition in 1799, the church stretched down almost to the river. Its neo-Classical replacement (1812–15) to the north-west, where Lamartine's burial service was held, is hugely dull. From it, however, you can walk across Mâcon's biggest public park, the Square de la Paix, with its massive war memorial, *belle-époque* roundabout and neat rosebeds, to the Hôtel-Dieu. The medieval hospital was originally in the Rue Carnot and only after much debate, so it is said, was the decision taken to build the replacement on the present site, where it was finished in 1770. Today the building serves as a psychiatric hospital, and visits have to be arranged with the major museum in Mâcon, the Musée des Ursulines, or with the medical authorities. You can usually get permission from the person at the main gate to see the central, domed chapel with its alternating frescos depicting the Old Testament prophets and scenes from the New Testament. The real attraction, however, is the pharmacy, complete with a remarkable collection of late eighteenth-century medicine pots, including two multicoloured jars nearly a metre tall, all in their original display cabinets.

Inevitably, given its modern function, the atmosphere in the Hôtel-Dieu and its gardens is sad. And this I think is the trouble with Mâcon as a whole. I have visited the town on several occasions in an attempt to work out why I find it less pleasing than, say, Tournus or Nevers. It is, I think, because Mâcon's buildings of real historic interest have had to assume modern administrative or medical duties. There *are* attractive features of the town, but you have to look for them: the beautifully restored house with an octagonal turret, now a lawyer's office, on the junction of the Rue de la Paroisse and the Rue Lamartine, for example, or the blind window built into the wall above a shop in the Rue Saint-Nizier. The doors, wider than most, are interesting too, and often open on to the long passages leading to *traboules* (such as we have already seen in Tournus and which are common in Lyon). These are internal courtyards with open stairways and galleries which provide light inside blocks of buildings (known as *îlots*) and ensure easy communication between different apartments. Many of the stairways have been walled in, but it is still possible to find some *traboules* more or less as they were three or four hundred years ago and to realize just how self-contained and inward-looking life was in these early high-density living conditions.

On Saturdays Mâcon hosts the biggest market in the region and its colourful, noisy atmosphere is another reminder, like the *traboules*, that the south of France is not far away. It is then that Mâcon comes alive and is probably much as it was early in the century, but the demands of modern development, the increase in tourist trade and the almost inevitable proliferations of pizzerias and crêperies have not, in my eyes at least, done Mâcon a service, whatever the commercial and financial rewards.

As you leave Mâcon to the south-west the horizon is soon dominated by the distinctive silhouettes of the great rocks of Solutré and Vergisson. In their shadow lie the villages noted for their celebrated (and frequently overpriced) dry white wine. Like their counterparts just a few kilometres further north, Pouilly, Loché and Fuissé, for example, are neat prosperous little communities, with every so often a real surprise, as the *vigneron*'s famous colonnaded house in Fuissé illustrates. Solutré is what attracts tourists to this corner of Burgundy, however. Excavations have revealed a human presence here going back to over 30,000 years ago, not in the form of permanent settlements but rather of temporary camps for hunters who lay in wait for the wild horses that migrated from the valley of the Saône, which they then slaughtered. Popular legend has long held that the horses were driven over the edge of the rock to their death 400 metres below, but modern examination of the huge depository of bones at

Solutré's base suggests this was not so. From a distance Solutré looks quite forbidding, but several paths provide relatively easy access to the craggy limestone summit, which juts out over the vines like the prow of a ship, in under half an hour – a fact that is proved by President Mitterrand's annual and much publicized walk on Whit Sunday. At its base is a museum, half-buried in the ground like a wartime bunker, where the history of the site is carefully and attractively explained. If you would like an easier walk, Vergisson is more gentle altogether.

Leaving the village of Vergisson the road climbs over a wooded hill before dropping down into Pierreclos, on a natural crossing point for routes from all directions. Its pale stone fifteenth-century château stands amid trees and vines on a spur of rock proudly fronting southwards towards Beaujolais. Just to the north is Milly-Lamartine and the pretty if modest eighteenth-century house where the poet spent most of his childhood. His deep attachment to Milly is evident from several of his poems and his memoirs, and when debts obliged him to sell the house in 1860 it was a blow from which some claim he never fully recovered. Just across the N79 is the rather dull Château de Monceau which Lamartine inherited in 1834 and where he frequently stayed until his death.

Instead of following the main road, a delightful way to begin heading west is by way of the narrow, twisting D212 which leaves the northern edge of Pierreclos and climbs up through forest and over the Col des Enceints at 529 metres, and just below the Croix Blanche nearly 100 metres higher. After Bourgvilain you cross the Grosne, but pay a brief visit to Berzé-le-Châtel with its massive fortified château built on a site once occupied by Romans and, because of its strategic position, a scene of several disputes throughout the Middle Ages. While unfortunately the château is not open to the public, the gardens are, in July and August. From these you have a good view of the biggest tower, the Tour du Boeuf, about which a popular tale is told of how long ago one of the owners had a bull and a man shut away without food to see who would live longer.

While at Berzé-le-Châtel it is worth dropping back down to Berzé-la-Ville to see the Chapelle des Moines, standing proudly on a spur of rock to the north-west of the village. In 1887 the local priest, who was interested in church décor, chipped away some plaster and uncovered part of a wall-painting of Christ. Encouraged by this, he continued and revealed the Romanesque frescos most of which can be seen today. Since 1947 the church has been listed as a historic monument and subject to much restoration. The frescos of principal interest are those in the apse. One group shows a figure of Christ in Majesty surrounded by groups of apostles, saints and bishops; another contains the unfortunate Agatha and other female saints. Individual scenes include one of St Vincent being roasted alive on a grill, watched by an imperturbable Roman official, and another of St Blaise being beheaded. Important and fine as they are today, it is easy to imagine how much more impressive they must have been once, when the faithful would have felt overwhelmed by the bright colours and details of this evidence of God's presence as soon as they walked into the church.

Immediately north from Berzé-le-Châtel is the road taking you back to Cluny and Cormatin. Caught between this (the D980) and the continuation of the N79 to Charolles is a ravishingly beautiful wedge of land, thickly wooded with oaks, beech, birch and pines, cut by nameless waterways draining west into the Arconce and Semence which meet at Charolles or east to the Grosne, and dotted with *étangs*, some of which towards Montceau-les-Mines are like small lakes, used in summer for boating and swimming. The land in this area is regularly around 500 metres above sea-level and almost every bend on the narrow, twisting roads presents a new and unexpected vista. Tiny villages, isolated churches, imposing châteaux all add to the charm. At Buffières, for example, the doorway to the château's stables bears an inscription in old Spanish which translates: 'Visitors are like fish; after three days they begin to smell'! Near by at Suin an outcrop of rocks rising to nearly 600 metres is topped by a huge statue of the Virgin Mary and offers a view which (local people say) takes in fifty belfries. I have never seen more than twenty, but the climb is certainly worthwhile. Saint-Bonnet-de-Joux has a small archeological museum displaying artefacts from Gallo-Roman and medieval times found in the region. Its château, on an outcrop of rock overlooking the Forêt d'Avaize, has remained the property of the same family for nearly 500 years.

You can visit the grounds and the magnificent seventeenth-century stables, which seem to me to have a distinctly Spanish design, though there is no specific reason for this as far as I have been able to discover. Northwards across the Bois de la Guiche and the Forêt du Rousset (there are panoramic views of these from the tiny hamlets of Saint Quentin and Le Martrat) the road climbs to Mont-Saint-Vincent at over 600 metres, for centuries a defensive point. Modern occupation is in the shape of meteorological and communications stations. Another archeological collection in what was the sixteenth-century salt store in the village is a reminder of the more distant past, and from the top of the hill it is easy to understand why this was one of the more important hill forts of the region. (It is worth noting that a section of the Grande Randonnée 7 links Saint-Vincent with Suin, a picturesque if quite demanding walk of about 25 kilometres.)

The granite chain – or spine, as it is known – which is essentially an extension of the ridge running down through the Côte d'Or, and of which Saint-Vincent is here the highest point, marks the beginning of the Charolais country. This large plain filling the south-west corner of the Saône-et-Loire *département* is bounded to the north by the Morvan and stretches away to the Loire. Huge areas of pasture offer grazing for the heavy, placid white Charolais cattle and in general agriculture has replaced the important industrial activity (coal, iron, ceramics) which developed here from the eighteenth century and for a while benefited from the opening of the Canal du Centre.

Charolles, its 'capital', is now far less active than it once was. The major cattle market takes place on the second and fourth Wednesday of the month, drawing dealers from a wide area, and there is an attractive general market every week, but the town is otherwise peaceful. Some *faïence* is produced too, but local people appear to see their economic future in tourism and for several years Charolles has been preparing itself, especially now that heavy traffic has been kept out of the town centre by the new bypass road.

Although the origins of the town's names are unknown, the general view is that it comes from a celtic word, *kadrigel*, meaning a fort near water. Throughout the Middle Ages the town belonged to the dukes of Burgundy, until Louis XI overcame its resistance and brought it under French royal jurisdiction. As a result of inter-marriages the region subsequently came under Austrian and Spanish influence (which no doubt explains the architectural style of the stables at Saint-Bonnet-de-Joux) until the late sixteenth century, but within another 150 years it had been fully reintegrated with France. The independent spirit of its people has had a more recent manifestation in the Resistance, and the town was awarded the Croix de Guerre in 1945.

As in Montargis, a series of pleasant walks has been devised along the banks of the rivers and canals, and an old mill on the Quai de la Poterne has been tastefully restored. What is left of the château now houses the town hall and an attractive public garden providing a good overview of the town and of one of the pepperpot towers of a ceramics factory. I once had a conversation with an elderly lady in this garden who complained about the damp climate and the fact that Charolles was slowly dying. Certainly this does not seem to be the case. In addition to the *quais*, streets and buildings of interest are well maintained. In what was the seventeenth-century Couvent de Visitadines, now a building which houses both a school and the law courts, there is a fine arcaded gallery. In the Rue du Prieuré are remains of a tenth-century building and of a later fifteenth-century octagonal tower, decorated with the coats of arms of local aristocratic families. And in the Rue du Calvaire is a tiny chapel known as Gros-Bon-Dieu, or more popularly as Gros-Caillou. Tradition has it that women who had been unfaithful to their husbands were obliged to clamber up the thirty-eight steps to its entrance with a large stone hanging from their neck!

No matter how hard it tries, however, Charolles will never be as popular with tourists as its near neighbour Paray-le-Monial, so called on account of the many religious communities to have existed there. One of the most popular postcard views of lower Burgundy is of the Basilique du Sacré-Coeur seen from the south, its splendid front complete with twin eleventh-century Romanesque towers (albeit of slightly different design) reflected in the waters of the Bourbince. As we have already noted, the church as a whole, which took 200 years to complete, is considered by experts to reflect more completely than any other in Burgundy the style of Cluny III. But it is not just for its picturesque qualities that people come to Paray in their tens of thousands. After Lourdes, Paray is the biggest pilgrimage centre in France for Christians, who come to pray at the shrine of Saint Marguerite-Marie Alacoque. Between 1673 and 1689 she is said to have had visions of Christ in which she was instructed to encourage devotion to his heart as a symbol of his love for mankind. The most significant result of this was the construction of the Sacré-Coeur in Paris, but a visit to almost any parish church in Catholic countries will reveal the extent of the cult's popularity in the form of votive offerings, especially during the last hundred years. (Records indicate that the first pilgrimage in 1873 drew over 100,000 people to Paray in a few weeks.) Marguerite-Marie was eventually canonized in 1920; her cell has been carefully restored and an effigy of her body lies above her mortal remains in an elaborate gilt and silver cask in the Chapelle de la Visitation.

Even if you are not attracted by such an example of highly charged religious emotion, a visit to the basilica church is obligatory. Balance and harmony are apparent everywhere, but nowhere more so than in the apse (despite the clutter of the inevitable souvenir shop just behind it) where the choir, the ambulatory with its elegant arches and slender columns, and the side chapels meet in a series of semi-circles. Above them rises the octagonal tower with its slate steeple over the crossing, on which the arches and decoration repeat those of the north tower of the main entrance. Inside there is much light and, as virtually everyone who has written about the church remarks, an apparent insistence on the Christian symbolism of the number three – three bays, three rows of windows, three aisles, for example. Whether this was by design or merely coincidental it is not possible to say, but there is something delightfully simple and essentially pure about the atmosphere of this church which distinguishes it (for me at least) from that of those in Tournus or even Vézelay and reflects more than mere architectural balance.

Only a dozen kilometres west of Paray is Digoin, surrounded by the Loire, the Arroux, the Canal du Centre and the Canal Latéral de la Loire. In the eighteenth century Digoin had no more than 1000 inhabitants and early in the twentieth around 6000; but by the 1990s this figure has grown to over 11,000. This extraordinary expansion is due partly to the wood trade, which has benefited from the transport facilities afforded by the canals, but more so to the development of a ceramics and pottery industry, now the most important in France, which exploits the different kinds of clay to be found in the Loire valley. As an interesting adjunct to this, the mid eighteenth-century building where the tourist office is housed contains, as well as the best documentation centre on the industry in France, an impressive array of artefacts from the pre-Gallo-Roman period to the present, and an illustrated account of the different manufacturing techniques to have been developed. Apart from the centre there is little of true historic interest in Digoin, though the aqueduct linking the two canals is an impressive feat of nineteenth-century engineering. With the exception of Dijon and possibly of Chalon-sur-Saône, no town in Burgundy has expanded at such a speed. The result is a rather unusual modern enclave in a region in which the past predominates, but to be fair to the *digoinais*, or to their town councils over the years, a genuine attempt has obviously been made to ensure that the building programme to meet the population expansion has been subject to controls. There are, it is true, some dull, functional buildings, but the Lycée 1970 and modern church are a tribute not only to architectural vision but to urban planning as well.

Digoin is one of several towns in a tract of land running north-eastwards, and embracing Gueugnon, Perrecy-les-Forges, Montceau-les-Mines, Blanzy and Le Creusot, which have developed in particular since the early years of the nineteenth century largely thanks to substantial and important coal deposits. (We should not forget that coal has been mined in this area from the Middle Ages.) Quarrying and metalworking have played their part too, and even if much of this activity has now ceased altogether or is on the wane, its echo remains in local names – La Tuilerie, Forges, Les Grosses Pierres, Le Fourneau or even L'Étang Noir.

In the main, industrial blight has destroyed much of what these towns have of historic interest. One important exception, however, is the Romanesque church of Saint-Pierre and Saint-Benoît at Perrecy-les-Forges, once part of a large priory. Though this is essentially a plain building, there is nonetheless some interesting and intriguing carving. The lintel above the main door bears an account of Christ's Passion; some of the figures of the disciples have disproportionately large heads and this naive technique is echoed in the northern bay of the porch where some odd hybrid animals, clearly intended to be elephants, have small boar tusks and cloven hooves. Rather more direct are two representations of lust in the form of a woman whose breasts are being attacked by snakes and by a mermaid whose twin tails are being held apart. There is also a carving of the scallop shell, traditionally the mark of the pilgrim route to Compostela and said to be the earliest example of its kind anywhere in the country.

From Perrecy all of the roads pass through countryside and suburban overspill dotted with pit heads and open-cast mines and, especially if you arrive from Cluny by way of Mont-Saint-Vincent, the contrast with much of the surrounding area is sharp and depressing. Montceau-les-Mines and Blanzy, whose populations have remained stable for the last hundred years, continue to exploit their natural wealth, but are also slowly adjusting to the challenge of cheaper sources of fuel from elsewhere and the demands of the late twentieth century. In winter the area is bleak and unforgiving, but central Montceau in summer has a modern brightness about it and has developed part of the canal into a *port de plaisance* which is both popular and attractive. Also popular, but a reminder of what working life was like for local people in only the recent past, is the restored mine (and industrial museum) of Saint-Claude in Blanzy.

Finally, close to the edge of the Morvan is Le Creusot, made famous throughout the world by the Schneider family who arrived from Lorraine in 1836, exploited the natural resources and created an industrial community which an early twentieth-century *Guide Bleu* of Burgundy describes with what now seems classic understatement as a '*ville toute neuve, mais souvent enfumée*'. Like the other towns in this group Le Creusot's industrial past goes back several hundred years, and before the development of the iron and steel industry it was an important glass-manufacturing centre. Faced with competition from the English, who had developed a technique for making crystal using coal, Louis XVI had the main factory in Sèvres, near Paris, moved to Le Creusot. In the 1780s the premises, built in the form of a château, began operating and continued to do so for about fifty years. In 1837 they were purchased by Eugène Schneider and over several generations were gradually developed into the hub of the family's empire. Occupied by the Germans during the War, the château was badly damaged by Allied bombing of the town in 1942 and 1943. The family undertook its restoration after the Liberation and eventually sold their vast enterprise to the Empain group, and the château and its grounds became absorbed into Le Creusot. A visit to the Château de la Verrerie offers an insight into the lifestyle of one of the most powerful industrial families in France during the last 200 years. Grandeur and hierarchy are everywhere. One of the former conical-shaped ovens has been converted into a private theatre based on La Scala in Milan and is decorated with scenes depicting life at the château during the previous century. In parts of the main building a museum contains examples of the Schneider achievements – some huge, like the locomotive 'La Gironde' – and the town is full of tributes to the family: statues, monuments, public buildings and even, in the church of Saint-Henri, a stained glass window with Henri Schneider as Saint-Eloi, patron saint of ploughmen and smiths. No doubt these tributes were entirely genuine. The Schneider family provided schools, hospitals, gymnasia, retirement homes and even a burial ground! A local story tells how in 1894 a young girl in one of the Schneider schools remarked to the lady of the great family of benefactors: *'Nous vous aimons Madame, comme une seconde mère envoyée par Dieu'*. The Schneiders' policy was paternalism at its most developed. But not far from the château, behind the railway station in the Rue Chaptal, is a row of miners' cottages. Now prettified for tourists and housing a small eco-museum, they nonetheless are a reminder of the way of life of some who were not quite so fortunate.

5
La France profonde

At the time of the general elections in France in 1981 which saw the socialists returned to government, the Party produced a poster depicting a village clustered around its church and etched against a clear blue sky. Together with its slogan, '*La Force tranquille*', it was clearly an appeal to traditional (some might even say conservative) values. This was indeed '*la France profonde*', beloved of the first socialist president of the Fifth Republic, François Mitterrand, whose relationship with the department of the Nièvre in various political roles dated from the Liberation and who, since 1959, had been mayor of Château-Chinon. On the edge of the Morvan and generally known as its capital, Château-Chinon itself – and indeed its immediate surroundings – has few if any of the features displayed on the poster, but for anyone who cares to look for them they are repeated endlessly throughout the secretive and entrancing *département* which spreads back west across to the valley of the Loire.

Together with the southern edge of the Puisaye and the smaller area known as the Bazois, the Nivernais is almost exactly in the middle of France. To the west is the Loire wandering along its wide valley, its surface frequently broken by large sand-banks and its waters significantly reduced both by the Canal Latéral between Briare and Digoin and by the demands of the thermonuclear reactors at Cosne. To the east is the Morvan, in a way a foretaste of the Massif Central away to the south, which effectively cuts off the region from the main Paris–Lyon axis and from many of the major Burgundian towns, notably Dijon. This relative geographical isolation – which will change significantly by the mid 1990s with the extension of the motorway to Montargis and the arrival of the TGV – is paralleled by a historical one as well. By the mid fourteenth century the region formed part of the territory under the control of Philippe le Hardi. Problems of administration compounded by others of succession meant that the Nivernais' history was rarely straightforward, however. After the fall of the Valois dynasty it became part of France, though no formal ratification or treaty was signed. Towards the end of the sixteenth century it fell under the control of the Gonzago family from Mantua in Lombardy before being sold in 1659 to that great and astute French statesman, Cardinal Mazarin. After the Revolution the duchy became a *département* and begin to experience steady if unspectacular economic growth. Within these general currents of history it has also been a kind of buffer zone and the scene of conflicts. During the Hundred Years War not a few châteaux were besieged by English troops; the Armagnacs and Burgundians frequently skirmished as each sought to gain control of the Loire and the Allier; the border with France, like that between Provence and the rest of the country, was for hundreds of years a site of potential conflict. It was this kind of threatening climate which resulted in so many fortified châteaux and farms being built: La Motte-Josserand just north of Donzy, Meauce south of Nevers or Chevenon just to the east. In later years, with stability and general peace, building, whether original or in the form of modifications, became altogether more elegant and open. The ducal palace in Nevers is widely considered to be the best example but there are others, as we shall see, like Bazoches south-east of Clamecy, or the Château de la Roche just to the north of Luzy. And no introduction to the region, however general and superficial, should fail to mention a more recent period when violence returned to the Nivernais, in the form of the Resistance. The remote areas and thick forests of the region provided ideal cover for those fighting against the Nazi occupation of France, and memorials – often no more than a clearing in woodland and a simple pile of stones – to various *maquis* are grim reminders of the cost of that struggle in human lives.

What Colette had to say about her native Puisaye remains true for parts of the northern strip of the Nivernais as well, but gradually the landscape begins to change. Although water is plentiful there are noticeably fewer ponds and *étangs*, while forests are both larger and more numerous, making the Nièvre one of the most thickly wooded *départements* in France. As with the area to the north, there is a marked change in landscape from west to east. The valley of the Loire gives way to a wooded plateau dominated by the immense Forêt des Bertranges, in turn followed by a more undulating landscape rising in places to 300 metres – and occasionally even higher, as at Montenoison (414 metres) – largely given over to pasture and the rearing of Charolais cattle. Further to the east is the narrow valley of the Aron which since the late eighteenth century has also provided the course for the Canal du Nivernais, linking the Yonne with the Loire which it joins at Decize. Thereafter the land begins to rise, particularly to the north and the Parc du Morvan. This gradual increase in altitude is matched by a decrease in population. The Loire valley provides living space for about two-thirds of the *nivernais* with almost a half of that proportion living in and around Nevers. Of the other towns which exploited local deposits of iron ore or coal – Guérigny, Fourchambault or Imphy, for example – and created important industrial centres in the nineteenth century, only the last has really maintained its position, thanks to a specialization in high-quality steel. Elsewhere, as in Cosne or Decize, a growth in numbers has been the result of a national policy of decentralization rather than of the development of industrial activity based on local resources. In fact, for more than a century now the question of the population of the Nièvre has been critical. Around 1900 an extraordinarily high number of people went to Paris where even menial jobs as servants and labourers were more remunerative than anything they could find locally. Recent statistics have shown, however, that the population had already been steadily decreasing during the previous decade or so and that this trend has continued at the rate, on average, of 1000 per year. But this is not due solely to local people moving away from the region. During the last twenty or thirty years many of the younger generation who have moved have been replaced by Parisians in search of a second or retirement home, and who have therefore increased the oldest, non-reproductive proportion of the population. While this is a problem which will probably be lessened with the planned improvement in road and rail communications, it is bound to remain serious for the foreseeable future.

Given both its history and the uneven population pattern, the Nièvre does not offer many important and interesting centres of any size distributed more or less at regular intervals as does the rest of Burgundy. La Charité-sur-Loire, Nevers and Clamecy automatically focus our attention, but the Nièvre is best explored otherwise almost at random. It remains a mixture of mystery and imagination, surprise and unexpected charm: tiny hamlets not much bigger than a substantial farm, châteaux of all ages – some ruinous, others impeccably restored – Romanesque churches, magnificent barns, pockets of forest and endless pastureland brilliantly coloured in spring with wild flowers – cowslips, lady's mantle, violets and wild orchids. Many of the bigger *étangs* are well looked after and popular with local fishermen, but just as many are left untended and are alive with frogs, fish and eels. The atmosphere of the Nièvre is special; often you have the impression of being in a society that has still not fully entered the twentieth century and which sustains only the most tenuous links with the surrounding regions. Nothing could be further removed from the prestigious villages of the Côte d'Or, the self-importance of Beaune or the bustle of Mâcon and Dijon, but Burgundy would be less complete without it, just as it would without them.

If you enter the Nièvre from Saint-Fargeau and Saint-Amand-en-Puisaye you cross the pretty valley of the Vrille and then follow a small tributary through woods to Saint-Vérain. Once heavily fortified, there remain on the west side of the village parts of the walls and of a massive thirteenth-century keep built by the local dukes who had fought in the early crusades. On their return they had the idea of turning their properties into a local Holy Land, a project of which we are reminded today by the tiny community called Jérusalem just to the west of the village. Saint-Vérain also has a rather plain but not unattractive church; the choir dates from the twelfth century, and there is some particularly fine stained glass.

From just beyond the château a minor road makes for Saint-Loup across slopes which were once covered with vines. Today production is small and what wine is made is not of any great quality, but at Saint-Loup, as at Saint-Père, there are cellars and some large presses to be seen which recall that the monks at the abbey Des Roches near Myennes were little different, in this one respect at least, from their brothers in Cîteaux or Tournus.

In these small villages you already have a taste of the special qualities of the Nièvre, and it comes as something of a surprise to find that Cosne-sur-Loire, on the confluence with the Nohain, is the second biggest town in the *département*, albeit with less than 13,000 inhabitants. There was a time when Cosne was known above all else as one of the most notorious places on the N7 for traffic jams, but since the opening of the bypass it has become much more peaceful and agreeable. In any case, the A6 motorway has reduced the amount of traffic carried by the national road.

The town's Roman name, Condate, meaning confluence, indicates that Cosne was already an important communication point in that period, and traces of a Roman road have been discovered here and at Saint-Loup. Throughout the Middle Ages, when it was largely under the control of the dukes of Nevers, Cosne was subject to a number of attacks from marauders who succeeded in crossing the Loire, but by the seventeenth century it benefited from the general peace and began to grow in size and importance. Some Italians attempted to develop a *faïencerie* to compete with those of Nevers, but met with limited success only; with the establishment of foundries from around 1660 using the waters of the Nohain to provide energy, however, Cosne changed from an artisanal centre to an early modern industrial one. In September 1677 Madame de Sévigné wrote to her daughter at Grignan in northern Provence about a visit she had paid to these foundries, describing them as, 'a real hell, the forges of Vulcan where eight or ten cyclops were making ships' anchors rather than swords for Aeneas'. The entrance to this '*véritable enfer*', the Forges de la

Chaussade, can be seen in the Rue des Forges where they remained until 1782, when they were transferred to Guérigny before being closed down altogether in 1971.

This industrial growth was much helped by the development of a road system at the end of the eighteenth century, the opening of a bridge in 1832 and the arrival thirty years later of the railway. (The present bridge dates from 1959, the previous one having been destroyed in an air-raid in June 1940.) Even though the foundries were removed, the encouragement of the steel industry continued in the twentieth century and several important factories have opened, creating employment and causing Cosne's population virtually to double since the 1950s. This industrial past is commemorated by a huge nineteenth-century crane and an anchor, made in 1861 and weighing over two and a half tonnes, both of which are on display along the Promenade des Marronniers. At the same time the town has not forsaken its more traditional past, and its markets on Sundays, Wednesdays and Fridays in the Halle aux Grains and its annual fairs (especially that of Saint Michael on 29 September) attract people from all areas and from both sides of the river. According to historic accounts and photographs of these events, people wore traditional dress especially for the occasion; this no longer happens, but the markets are an important outlet for artisanal workers and for local peasant farmers in particular and are an essential feature of life in this part of the Nièvre.

The public buildings in Cosne are of relatively little interest, though the church of Saint-Agnan, on the site of a former Cluniac priory and much restored, has some attractive and unusual features. Of these, the handsome gateway (uncovered in 1974) opposite the main entrance has a tympanum decorated with angels and griffins and an image of a nun receiving a sword from Saint John, probably symbolizing the establishment of the order. A glimpse of the town's original fortifications can be had in the form of the Tour Fraicte and a small covered arcade from the sixteenth century exists in the Rue Saint-Agnan. An interesting archeological collection, particularly good in respect of ceramics and mosaics, is on display in the Maison des Chapelains, a sixteenth-century house with some finely carved ceilings. And for anyone interested in the peasant and artisanal life of the area it is worth making the short journey north to Celle-sur-Loire where there is a small but excellent Musée des Traditions Paysannes containing tools, costumes, furniture and so on, all presented in a large barn in the form of reconstructed scenes from peasant life.

From Cosne, initially along the valley of the Nohain which can be surprisingly high in winter, the road leads to Donzy lying in a shallow valley surrounded by farmland and forests. Just to the north is the château of La Motte-Josserand. Architecturally little has changed here for 450 years. Apart from the opening of some windows, the outside with its gun and arrow slits and fortified doorway is forbidding, and, once surrounded by a moat (controlled by an intricate system of sluice-gates), it must have been virtually impregnable. It is now open to the public, and inside a wooden gallery, reached by stairways cut in the thickness of the walls, provides access to the upper rooms. Above the gateway is a small chapel and on the north-west side a vast room contains a monumental fireplace. The château is one of the best examples of its kind in this part of the Nièvre.

Donzy itself bears few traces of an important and turbulent past, especially in the Middle Ages when local overlords resisted the attempts of both the bishops of Auxerre and the dukes of Nevers to take control of them. But on the south side, down a poorly signposted road leading to Presle and which rejoins the Nohain, is Donzy-le-Pré, where there are the remains (under restoration) of the twelfth-century priory of Notre-Dame. The tympanum bearing an effigy of Mary with Jesus, flanked by the kneeling figures of the prophet Isaiah and the angel Gabriel, is a small version of the one over the main door of Chartres cathedral. Above Mary's head the hand of God descends in blessing.

Beyond the ruins a narrow road to Lyot leads over a hill and past a quarry to Suilly-la-Tour, a gem for anyone wishing to see a typical local community. Some houses have been renovated, others wait for people with either sufficient money or time. The local stone is pale cream in colour, softer than the darker, mottled stone used only a few kilometres further north. Some of the houses are *résidences secondaires* but there is an air of activity here as well. Tools are propped against walls, piles of logs are regularly replenished, chickens wander at will. And in Presle on the banks of the Nohain is the local château, dating from the fourteenth and sixteenth centuries and with an ornate main gate bearing the date 1605. Ten years ago the château was in large part ruined. The present owner has restored virtually all of it, rebuilding chimneys, reroofing the main wing on the west side and renovating other parts. In the south wing is a chapel with frescos dating from the late fifteenth century. While the château is not officially open to the public the *gardienne*, whose house is by the main gate, will show you round, and only then do you fully realize, as at Tanlay or Ancy-le-Franc, the cost of taking on a project of this kind. Even with some assistance from the state, to restore a site of this size is a mammoth financial undertaking. The owners, who live in Paris, come here during the winter for the hunting season and again for the summer. To help finance the venture the grounds and one of the outbuildings are now used for receptions and the result is the transformation of a fine vaulted cellar into a modern bar, while the magnificent room above has become a banqueting hall furnished with plastic-topped tables and with whitened walls festooned with sets of antlers and the stuffed heads of some of the unfortunate creatures killed in the surrounding woods. But short of unlimited private capital or huge state support there is no alternative. The solution here is different from those found at Ratilly or at Saint-Fargeau, but just as necessary.

Before moving further south to the vineyards around Pouilly and the thick forest of Bertranges, Clamecy in the north-eastern corner of the *département* is worth a visit. From Donzy one road passes through Entrains, the site of important Gallo-Roman settlements of which much evidence has been uncovered over the past twenty years and distributed rather thoughtlessly to museums all over France. A second passes by way of Menou with its elegant late seventeenth-century château, totally different from those at La Motte and at Corbelin just 3 kilometres further on, and continues between the forests of Couets and d'Arcy and down the valley of the Sauzay to Corvol-l'Orgueilleux, so named after a twelfth-century nobleman. Evidence of occupation from early history through Gallo-Roman times and the Middle Ages make this an interesting village to visit. It grew in the nineteenth century on account of the wood trade and is still active today even though it is largely overshadowed by Clamecy.

From the sixteenth century Clamecy owed economic growth to wood. Here logs from the Morvan were made into huge rafts (like those on the Saône) which went by the Yonne and the Seine to Paris. The opening of the Canal du Nivernais and the competition from barges caused considerable hardship and unrest among the *flotteurs* who had already expressed their discontent on several occasions during the eighteenth century in the form of strikes and riots. While this method of transporting logs died out with rail and road links (though it is remembered in the local sweets known as *bûchettes* or little logs), wood still provides the basis for local industry. As in Prémery, local factories treat it chemically for the extraction of different essences and charcoal is produced and sold worldwide. But with its agreeable site on a promontory at the confluence of the Beuvron and the Yonne, the proximity of the Morvan and improved communications, Clamecy has become much more a tourist and cultural centre.

The centre of the old town, officially protected as being of historic interest, recalls that of Sens and is dominated by the ornate, square tower of Saint-Martin. All around are pleasant, well-maintained streets with timbered houses with their tiny courtyards and stairways and several fine doorways and windows. One curiosity, in the Rue de la Monnaie, is the tiny carving of a crouched figure with hands clasped across his chest, generally thought to be of Saint Ytrope, whose effigy is to be found on the medieval route to Compostela. In the Rue Bourgeoise is the Centre Culturel Romain-Rolland, containing a collection of the writer's possessions and a number of special editions of his novels. In the basement the vaulted cellars, which continue underneath the street to join those below the town's museum, are in frequent use as an exhibition centre.

Another historical curiosity at Clamecy is the story concerning the area around the church of Notre-Dame de Bethléem on the banks of the Yonne. In the twelfth century Guillaume IV, Comte de Nevers, founded a hospital here. When in 1168 he fell ill while fighting in the Holy Land he asked to be buried in Bethlehem and as a mark of his gratitude willed the hospital in Clamecy to the Christian church there so that it could be used as a place of refuge should the Christians find themselves driven out by the Moslems. In 1223 this is precisely what happened, and from 1225 until the Revolution fifty bishops of Bethlehem had their residence in the heart of France. Their names are inscribed on a cenotaph inside the modern (1927) church.

To return towards Donzy it is worth trying to pick a route back across the Forêt des Couets and the Bois des Forts by way of tiny, almost lost hamlets grouped around a natural crossing point or in the shelter of a valley — Buzy le Buisson on the Sauzay, Colméry or Cessy-les-Bois, for example. As you emerge from the forested area south of Donzy you will notice Sancerre on its hill just beyond the west bank of the Loire, rising above the surrounding patchwork of vineyards. On the east, too, as the land slopes down on average by 70 metres or so, arable land gives way to vines producing the grapes for the white wine sold under the label of Pouilly-Fumé, so called on account of the slightly smoky taste it can have at times. To merit this *appellation* the wine must be made entirely from Sauvignon Blanc grapes; the less tasteful Chasselas is also produced in considerable quantity and goes into an inferior, though not unpleasant, and inexpensive alternative. Once it was overshadowed by its more illustrious neighbour across the river, but Pouilly-sur-Loire now produces wine which is in demand and no longer as cheap as it once was. Nonetheless it is still very competitively priced in comparison with the 'other' Pouilly wines from just south of Mâcon and is in general a much more reliable wine than Chablis. There is an excellent wine fair here in the middle of August, and the *cave co-opérative* just south of the village centre is modern and promotes itself well; the staff are friendly and the tastings generous. There are plenty of smaller independent producers as well, especially in the strip of land between the N7 and the river in villages like Bois-Gibault or Tracy. On the outskirts of the latter is an ornate multi-pinnacled château which was acquired in the late sixteenth century by François Stutt, whose ancestors were related to the royal family of Scotland. His descendants still live here.

La Charité-sur-Loire, set in a shallow depression on the river bank, is reached via the N7 in a few minutes. Evidence of some form of habitation dating from the second century has been discovered here, but La Charité's meaningful history probably began 500 years later. Originally called Seyr, which according to legend and some information in the Square des Bénédictins appears to have meant 'town in the sun', the community was established around a monastery dedicated to the Virgin Mary in the seventh century and subsequently destroyed by the Normans. Excavations in the 1970s indeed uncovered remains of what was probably a Carolingian church, but it seems probable that the town became fully established from the mid eleventh century when Hugues, abbot of Cluny, founded the first priory which quickly developed a network of dependent churches and convents across France and beyond into the rest of Europe. The town's present name originates from the amount of charity given to the poor in these early years and the priory's own coat of arms is of three open golden bags on a blue background.

During the wars of religion the town suffered a great deal; in particular in 1573, when the Huguenots were massacred after a siege which had lasted for twelve months. Such violence as this and damage from several major fires, notably one in 1559, have meant that much of what must have been a substantial and elegant medieval town has disappeared. The monastery and its church in particular hardly enjoyed a better fate. Although worthy attempts have been made in the past to rescue the town from falling into total ruin, notably by Colbert in the seventeenth century and by the nineteenth-century writer and politician Prosper Mérimée, they have not been wholly successful, and the task confronting the national and departmental authorities today is daunting. Quite reasonably, most attention is being paid to the monastery church, and it is now possible to examine parts from the different building periods between 1059 and 1135 and the subsequent attempted restorations. Even though a great deal has been lost, it is relatively easy to gain a sense of the original size of the church, which would have come close to that of Cluny III.

Whether or not it was deliberate or indeed whether it would have been the case eight and a half centuries ago is impossible to say, but when you stand at the crossing of Notre-Dame the perspectives are such that you have the impression of seeing far beyond the church as though it were open to the world. Of the detailed work that has been preserved, the best is a tympanum originally from the west façade and now inside the church which shows Christ (looking remarkably happy) between Moses and Elijah above a scene depicting the presentation of Christ in the temple and another of the adoration of the three kings, with a decidedly anxious looking Joseph standing behind Mary's chair.

Outside the church the excavations have now uncovered various parts of the monastery – refectory, cellars, kitchen, for example – and the buildings in the Cour du Prieuré on the north side have been restored by a wine merchant. From here, a short walk up the steep grass bank to the Promenade des Remparts and the remaining round fourteenth-century tower, La Tour de Cuffy, allows you a good impression of the full extent of the original buildings, and fine views over the roofs of La Charité and in both directions along the Loire.

Perhaps rather like Nuits-Saint-Georges, La Charité has suffered from the proximity of more important or prestigious towns. Nevers clearly dominates the area as it has for centuries, but Cosne too has grown in stature with its industrial activity. Old photographs of La Charité show busy river scenes with barges bearing logs, and older accounts of the town's commercial life describe a *faïencerie* and an active trade in salt, wine, jewellery, buttons and ironmongery (*quincaillerie*). Echoes of this remain in street names, like that of Rue du Grenier du Sel, now sadly in a bad state of preservation. And throughout the town are examples of some fine medieval houses clearly indicative of a prosperous past. Today, like so many towns in the Nièvre, it has to rely almost solely on tourists to fuel the local economy. Gradually, however, La Charité appears to be emerging from years of being overlooked if not completely neglected, and that is something to be welcomed.

Immediately to the east of La Charité lies the vast expanse (nearly 10,000 hectares) of the Forêt des Bertranges, which formed part of the monastery's land until it was confiscated and given to the state after the Revolution. Rich in iron ore, this whole area was exploited well into the nineteenth century, producing several thousand tonnes of iron of different grades each year. The charcoal needed to fire the forges was easily obtainable and the industry thrived. None of this activity continues today, but in many if not most of the communities scattered across the plateau are remains of forges and workers' houses. The wood trade still flourishes and huge sawmills at places like Murlin provide building material for the entire country, but the forest is now promoted for recreational and leisure activities and protected as an area of natural beauty. Its main trees are oaks, beeches and pines, many of them one and even two hundred years old. The focal point is the Rond de la Réserve, easily reached from the village of Raveau, and the pretty *étang* with its spring known as La Vache. From the Rond, a meeting place for six forest tracks and the Grande Randonnée 3, a series of marked paths in the form of loops bring you back to the starting point – and your car. This is something which has always seemed to me to be a contradiction. With the agreement of the national *foot*paths society the main tracks are open to cars as well. You are asked to respect nature, not to pollute the atmosphere and to enjoy being able to escape from the noise of the town. And yet . . . There is nothing more annoying than having to move out of the way as yet another estate-car full of potential picnickers decides to take advantage of this (to me) bizarre aberration.

If you do drive across the forest you eventually meet the valley of the Nièvre, which follows a shallow fault line across the plateau and is a natural *bassin* for the dozens of tiny streams from both sides. By Guérigny, where its water was channelled to provide energy for the national foundries, it becomes quite broad before splitting up into two main streams which do not reunite until just outside Nevers. Although Guérigny has done its best to turn an industrial past into something of historic and archeological interest for the visitor, it remains rather drab. Time should be taken, however, to see the Château de Villemenant, on the road leading past the old foundries to La Quellerie, which belonged to the Veaulce family who owed their fortune to the iron industry. Subject to much restoration and change over 500 years, it is a well-maintained building surrounded by pleasant gardens, and a particularly good example of the way in which a château primarily concerned with defence could be transformed into an elegant residence. Its steeply pitched roof is reputed to have the finest example of a vaulted beam structure — made from chestnut — in the whole of the *département*.

Rather than heading for Nevers by the main road, it is worth crossing the river and following the narrower one which skirts the edge of the Forêt des Bertranges as far as Urzy. Here you will find the seventeenth-century classical summer residence of the bishops of Nevers; surrounded as it is by water, it must, one imagines, have been regularly flooded in winter and spring. (In summer mosquitoes must have been a problem as well.) The road then continues to join the main D117 at the bridge, the Pont Saint-Ours. Its name has nothing to do with bears but it is said to derive from the miracle in the sixth century when one Aré, a priest from Nevers, brought back to life his friend Ours who had been drowned in a sudden flood.

Nevers

Whatever speculation there has been about Nevers' origins, there can be no doubt that its site from the earliest times was ideal for settlement. On the confluence of the Nièvre and the Loire and only a few kilometres upstream from the mouth of the Allier, the opportunities for communications and trading are obvious. The link with the Canal Latéral de la Loire, the arrival of the railways and the road connections by way of the N7 (even though as at Cosne the reduction in traffic has been significant) have ensured that in more recent years this has continued. The emphasis may have changed. *Faïence* is still a speciality — indeed Nevers is one of the most celebrated sources in France — and heavy engineering work continues in the national railway works centre, but a whole new light-industrial estate has developed bringing much-needed employment to the region. The adoption of the car-racing circuit at Magny-Cours 20 kilometres to the south for the international Formula One competition has also had a very considerable impact on the local economy. The result of this continued activity has been that the town's population has grown by about a third since the 1950s and, though challenged hard by Auxerre, Nevers is the third largest and most significant town in Burgundy after Dijon and Chalon.

Without question the best view of the town is, as with Auxerre, from the bridge to the south. Immediately ahead are the cathedral and ducal palace and, while there are fewer spires and belfries than there once were (which gave Nevers the nickname of '*la ville pointue*'), the skyline remains attractive. Unfortunately, having survived for centuries relatively unscathed, Nevers was the target for a fierce bombing raid in July 1944 and many buildings were severely damaged. But restoration has been steady and, before he committed suicide in May 1993, the mayor Pierre Bérégovoy had succeeded in imparting his own enthusiasm and sense of pride in Nevers to his fellow citizens at large.

The earliest recorded name of a settlement here is Noviodunum Aeduorum and it marked the southern edge of territories belonging to the Gaulish tribe, the Aedui. By the third century Christianity had been established and within a further 300 years a bishop was in place, attached to Autun. From the thirteenth century Nevers fell under the jurisdiction of a series of different noble families, including those of Flanders and of Mantua. (Nevers is twinned with the Lombardy town today.) By then the first fortifications had been built and, strong and wealthy, the town was made into a duchy in 1538.

This emergence of Nevers as an influential power was symbolized by the century-long building (1464–1565) of the ducal palace, of which different features reflect different political climates. Thus on the north side the round towers appear to be far more suited to a defensive château, while on the south, where the façade looks down to the river across what is now the Place de la République, the architecture is altogether more elegant and conciliatory. Its three octagonal towers, of which the central one is carved with coats of arms and with legends concerning the Clèves family, are its most striking feature. The windows rise from right to left following the inner stairways and the whole building is topped by pinnacles, chimneys and outshot windows, whose ornamentation echoes that of the main tower. Much of this work, with its clear italianate influence, was that of the Gonzago family. For all its external elegance, however, what was self-evidently a corresponding richness on the inside of the palace has surrendered to the demands of modern bureaucracy, and there is an interesting contrast to be made here with the fate of parts of the Palais des Ducs in Dijon and with the prefectural offices in Auxerre.

From the Place Ducale and Place de la République, overlooked by several houses from the seventeenth century, you can follow the path of the dukes as they went for their boats down the steps in the Montée des Princes. The view from here is good but it would be even better were it not for the hideously ugly Maison des Sports et de la Culture, with its seven stories of dull concrete. Fortunately it has been earmarked for eventual demolition.

West of a line down to the river from the ducal palace lies what is known as the *ville haute*, the area clustered around the hillock on top of which is the Cathédrale Saint-Cyr-et-Sainte-Julitte. Over 100 metres long, the church is a mixture of different architectural styles from the eleventh to the sixteenth centuries, one particularly unusual feature being that it has two apses, one at each end. The Romanesque one to the west covers the site of a Roman temple and baptistry. The air-raids of 1944 revealed evidence of these and it is now possible to inspect parts both of the original bath and of a Carolingian one constructed several centuries later. Inside the cathedral this apse is decorated with a faded twelfth-century fresco of Christ surrounded by the different symbols of the evangelists and the Old Testament prophets. In the crypt beneath is a representation of the Laying in the Tomb, dating probably from the fifteenth century. Such was the general damage to the cathedral in 1944 that much of the original decoration has disappeared but at the base of the columns in the triforium you can see carvings of a whole range of people taken from all walks of life: monks, merchants, peasants and so on. One is depicted playing with a ball, which would have been a leather bag stuffed with bran, in a game known locally as *soule*.

South from the cathedral a series of narrow cobbled streets with some elegant town houses lead down to the river and the busy Place Mossé, the junction for traffic coming across the river. Just past a row of neat one-time port-workers' houses on the Quai des Mariniers you come to the fifteenth-century Tour Goguin, at the southern end of the section of the fortifications leading up to the Porte du Croux. To the west of these are some pleasant public gardens and to the east part of Notre-Dame, the seventh-century Benedictine abbey for nuns, of which a later thirteenth-century chapter house still stands and is now used for small exhibitions and gatherings of local societies. The Porte du Croux, an excellent example of a fortified gate topped with look-out turrets and battlements and the most impressive part of Nevers' defences to be seen today, now houses a modest archeological museum and is next door to the town's principal *faïencerie*, which has been on the same site for nearly four centuries. It was founded by Italian craftsmen brought to Nevers by the Gonzago family, and you find here *faïence* of a quality (and at a price) to rank with the best from Moustiers in Provence. By the seventeenth century there were as many as a dozen factories employing nearly 2000 workmen, their ware more richly decorated than that from the Midi, often with groups of people or scenes of Chinese inspiration. A collection is to be found in the Musée Municipal.

The Porte du Croux marks the western limits of the medieval town and you meet the north-western corner just a couple of hundred metres away in what is now Nevers' main commercial axis, the Avenue Général de Gaulle, which to the left leads to the railway station. Before cutting back across the centre to discover the so-called *ville basse* around the church of Saint-Étienne, a glance at the Rue Vertpré is not amiss. Developed since the eighteenth century, this grey, rather unprepossessing street contains a number of houses which have undergone thoughtful restoration and is a good indicator of Nevers' growing prosperity.

From the Place Carnot, the social hub of Nevers, just north of the ducal palace, the Rue Saint-Martin (named after an eighth-century abbey) leads down to the Rue du Commerce. It is difficult to imagine this as the main route through Nevers before World War II (in fact a continuation of the N7) with traffic 'flowing' in both directions. Since 1980 it has been a pedestrian area, with some of Nevers' most expensive shops, and is busy in a different way. You are now above an area of the town famed as well for its vast network of cellars, some of them double, which in the past enabled people to move about and also, it is said, provided potential escape routes down to the banks of the river. Above ground the Place Guy Coquille and the Rue Saint-Étienne lead to the church, set back in a small square and now thought to have been built at the very end of the eleventh century on the site of a seventh-century monastery. If the cathedral (through no fault of its own) is a mixture of styles and periods, Saint-Étienne, miraculously having escaped bomb damage, is rightly recognized as one of the purest and most homogeneous examples of Romanesque architecture of its period. Both outside and in it is virtually devoid of decoration and while there are signs of an earlier door the present one matches the severity of the west façade perfectly. To the rear the apse presents a beautifully proportional cluster of three chapels with their simple arched windows and buttresses and the grassed area around the church (rather too regularly visited by local dogs for some people's liking) covers a former cemetery remembered in the rather macabrely named Rue Charnier.

With its many timbered houses, ornate doorways, cobbled streets and alleyways, and the remains of a host of religious communities, the rest of the centre of Nevers deserves further exploration. And for a leisurely stroll there are, as well as the gardens by the Porte du Croux, lawns down to the river from the ducal palace, the Parc Roger Salengro with its ancient elm and lime trees, lawns, flower-beds and paths, and beyond that the convent of Saint-Gildard, complete with a replica of the grotto at Lourdes.

From Nevers the N7 continues directly south, leaving the N81 to follow the valley of the Loire through the little street town of Imphy to Decize, now an equally important industrial centre with a rubber factory, a ceramics works and a medical centre. Its site is rather odd, since the centre of the old town is on a small chalky island which bears fragments of the fortifications built between the twelfth and fifteenth centuries. At the confluence of the Loire, the Vieille Loire, the Aron, and the canals of both the former and of the Nivernais, the larger modern conglomeration of Decize which takes in Faubourg Saint-Privé and Saint-Léger-des-Vignes on the slopes to the north has a series of bridges which make it possible to cross back and forth and appreciate how the area has developed over the centuries. Decize is a thriving community and its residents, workers and visitors alike enjoy, during the summer months at least, the excellent recreational facilities which the town has developed, in particular the Stade Nautique on the Loire. And even if it is of no great historic interest, the Promenade des Halles is worth anyone's time. On the spit of land between the Aron and the Loire, this is a 900-metre walk between soaring plane and lime trees, some of which are reputedly well over 200 years old.

Beyond Decize through Luzy to the departmental boundary with Saône et Loire the road begins to climb and twist as it crosses the lower approaches to the Morvan. To the south the landscape offers a mixture of poor wet soil, rich grasslands and woods, sprinkled with *étangs* of various sizes, farm buildings and substantial houses, many in a semi-ruinous condition. This gradually gives way to the higher area rich in the coal and iron ore on which the various industrial communities on the way to Montceau-les-Mines were developed. But a far more interesting route leads directly north from Decize through the Forêt des Minimes. After 10 kilometres is the small town of La Machine, named in this plain, unimaginative way after equipment for extracting coal which was installed in the seventeenth century. As might be expected, La Machine is hardly attractive, but it is a good starting point for walks and excursions north along the top of the Côtes du Nivernais ridge, at an average height of around 350 metres and rising in places (*les buttes*) to over 400, towards either Saint-Saulge or Prémery, barely 20 kilometres to the west. Although no major Randonnée crosses this region, it is easily explored by any number of departmental and local paths or by tracks through thick, dank forests and across beautiful undulating pastureland, grazed by the ubiquitous creamy-white Charolais and spotted with clumps of wild prunus which in spring look as though they are covered in snow.

Saint-Saulge is pretty, with some medieval houses and a sixteenth-century church containing richly coloured stained glass of the same period. But it is also renowned, especially locally, for amusing tales. Most countries tell belittling stories about the inhabitants of another – the English about the Irish, the Germans about the Austrians, the French about the Belgians. Whatever the origins of the local stories, it seems the Saint-Saulgeois were the butt of their neighbours. One tells of how when grass was discovered growing from the top of the church tower a cow was taken up there to keep it grazed. Another has the members of the village council waiting with their mouths open beneath a plum tree; whoever has a plum fall into his mouth is automatically elected mayor. Yet another recounts how donkeys must not be allowed to see the reflection of the moon in an *étang* in case they drink it and it disappears for ever. If they were once offended by such stories, however, local inhabitants are happy enough now to have illustrations of them sold in the form of postcards.

From Saint-Saulge the main road cuts through the Bois-de-Saint-Franchy, past the village of the same name and then Lurcy-le-Bourg, with a twelfth-century church and parts of a fifteenth-century Cluniac priory now incorporated in a large working farm. Thereafter the road crosses farmland and drops down gently to Prémery and the valley of the Nièvre. But this is virtually the very centre of the *département* and it is infinitely rewarding to select almost at random any of the minor side roads (often with grass pushing through the asphalt) to explore communities which are usually no more than a collection of farm buildings. In places the farms are still active but elsewhere they have been rescued from ruin only by being purchased as second or retirement homes by Parisians, and even by British people willing to commit themselves to a deeply rural lifestyle and enjoy a climate which, while rather more extreme, is not significantly different from their own. In fact the only occasional blot on the horizon in this region is the smoke from the charcoal factory at Prémery. The busy little town whose name means 'near the river' was once another of the places favoured by the bishops of Nevers from the fourteenth to seventeenth centuries for their summer retreat. Of their château a wing and two towers — including that of the main entrance — remain and, well restored, are used by the local municipality. A hundred metres or so away and just off the main street stands the church of Saint-Marcel which is noted for a statue of the Virgin Mary considered to have been made probably by one of Claus Sluter's pupils in Dijon. Local activities are much encouraged here and a walking club offers a whole series of excursions in the immediate vicinity. A particularly attractive one takes in

Giry with its immaculate fourteenth-century château and forest with oak trees said to be a century older still, Arthel and the Butte de Montenoison. Named after a local tribe, the Onesii, this hill, 410 metres high, offers one of the best panoramic views across the Nièvre in all directions especially to the east towards the Morvan where, on a clear day, the white modern church of Lormes can be seen. So advantageous did the dukes of Nevers consider the site to be that they built a château on it but only a few ruins now remain. Six hundred years later Montenoison came into its own again as a stronghold of the Nièvre's Resistance fighters.

From Prémery, the western edge of the Morvan is reached easily by returning by way of Saint-Saulge and thereafter by taking the road from Nevers to Château-Chinon. After Châtillon-en-Bazois, where it crosses the Aron and the Nivernais canal, the road climbs through a forest largely of oaks and pines past Saint-Péreuse and Dommartin. Just south of the main road after the turning to Saint-Péreuse is a small road leading to the Château de Saulières and the Étang de l'Île. Set back on a terrace and sheltering against the trees is an elegant eighteenth-century building quite unusual in this part of Burgundy and resembling châteaux to be found much nearer Paris. Unfortunately it is not open to the public, but it is possible to skirt the gardens and walk down to the *étang* where forest paths allow you to explore the forest of Saulières and eventually lead you either north and back to the main road or south to Moulins-Engilbert. But a more interesting and picturesque route after Saint-Saulge is via Aunay-en-Bazois, where in summer the château's courtyard is resplendent with orange trees, and beyond to Niault, perched on a rocky spur and overlooking the valley of the Veynon. Immediately north are dense woods and a most attractive road to Blismes. East, and equally attractive, another leads to Saint-Hilaire and Château-Chinon. One particularly good way of appreciating the scenery of this corner of the Nièvre is by train. At Tamnay-en-Bazois there are three possible journeys. One allows you to follow the valley of the Aron down to Decize; another hugs the forested escarpment before branching north-west for Corbigny (where incidentally there is an excellent weekly market); and yet another follows the contours of the southern edge of the Morvan through

Niault at around 400 metres, and offers a splendid panoramic view across to Saulières and to Saint-Léger-de-Fougeret where the hills rise 200 metres higher.

And so to the Morvan itself.

6
In and around the Morvan

When the Romans established themselves in Provence and began to move north towards Lyon and beyond they carefully avoided the Mont Ventoux. With its harsh terrain and changeable climate it seemed to them to be a mysterious, threatening place, and a superstition grew that it was the entry to the underworld. Although no such story appears to be associated with the Morvan, it does derive its name from the Celtic *mor'ven* meaning the 'black mountain' and its weather, if less fickle than that around Ventoux, can be harsh and even violent. While from certain angles the Morvan appears almost mountainous, it is in fact a plateau rising gently from north to south on a huge outcrop of granite. Certainly it is an imposing feature on the skyline, its blackness the effect of the forests which, even at quite close range, can seem defensive and impenetrable.

The Morvan owes its identity entirely to geographical and topographical features. It has no political or administrative existence which could mark it out from *départements*, for example; in fact, while it is substantially in the Nièvre it straddles the other three Burgundian *départements* as well. After considerable and not always amicable discussion, in 1970 it was given the status of a *parc régional*, of which there are twenty-three in France; it is one of the biggest and most popular. About 175,000 hectares in size, it covers an area inside a 'boundary' which could be drawn from Avallon on the north side to Lormes and Château-Chinon on the west, south to Saint-Honoré-les-Bains and Autun, and then north to Saulieu. It reaches its highest point at Haut-Folin (901 metres) in the south-eastern corner, where in general the terrain becomes much more rugged and even inhospitable, and where there are other important hills such as Mont Beuvray (796 metres) and Mont Préneley (855 metres) as well as gorges and waterfalls.

Water in various forms gives the Morvan much of its particular character. On average the region has six months' rain and snow each year – according to many Burgundians elsewhere it rains every day! This soaks through a sponge-like topsoil, created by centuries of weathering of the rock's surface and rotting vegetation, and reaches the impervious surface of the granite mass beneath, resulting both in areas of marshy land known locally as *mouilles* and surface water (*mortes-eaux*), and in a multitude of springs, streams and waterfalls. During the winter and spring months these are swollen by seasonal rain and melting snow, and what is a quiet, pretty waterway in July or August can quickly become a raging torrent. In turn the streams drain into larger rivers including the Yonne, which rises just by Mont Préneley. To the south-east the Terrin, La Celle and Méchet feed the Arroux, which flows into the Loire at Digoin. Several of these rivers, notably the Cure and the Serein flowing northwards, played important roles in the transportation of logs in the form of rafts (as on the Saône) in the direction of Paris. For several centuries a system of sluices controlled the flow of water from swampy areas, increasing it when extra 'power' was needed, but eventually it was decided that lakes could do this job more effectively. The first to be created was Les Settons (*séton* means swamp) and by 1858 the necessary dam had been completed, but its effectiveness was short-lived as methods of transport changed. Of the six major lakes (all artificial) the others date from the twentieth century. They are still important for regulating the amount of water in the Yonne, are used for the generation of hydro-electric power and provide drinking water for thousands, humans and cattle alike. They also attract tourists and in the summer accommodate water-sports of all kinds. Some people find that they do not blend easily with the typical Morvan landscape, but apart from the dams themselves and the buildings housing the necessary machinery, such a judgement seems to me to be exaggerated. In the southern and highest part of the *parc régional*, snow has encouraged the installation of some small ski-lifts and the opening of a series of cross-country routes.

While with the exception of the gentler slopes to the north the Morvan has little cultivable land – and indeed the quality of the soil is generally poor – the amount of rain does encourage the growth of grass, wild flowers and trees. Even so, pasture is not as rich as that to the west in the heart of the Nièvre, and while Charolais cattle are reared here (a single beast needs at least two hectares) after eighteen months or two years most are moved elsewhere for fattening. But for the visitor the general impression of the Morvan itself is of a vast island of green, alive in spring with wild flower such as hyacinths, aconites, violets, foxgloves, heathers, daffodils and even orchids. This impression is created as much by trees as by grass, and especially by pines and firs, though oak, beech, chestnut and birch are still more plentiful and provide relief particularly in autumn when their dying leaves create splashes of colour against a dark background. Conifers are, of course, on the increase, since they can be farmed to meet the continuing demand for building material, charcoal and Christmas trees. But their presence is slowly changing the quality and nature of the undergrowth in certain areas and those who value the Morvan as a special natural region are understandably beginning to show some concern.

That wood should still be commercially viable is important, however, for while a growth in tourism has resulted in considerable income it has also brought its attendant damage and threat of pollution. (Well over 10,000 visitors to the Lac des Settons have regularly been recorded on 15 August alone!) But more than this, the nature and climate of the Morvan have never been conducive to any life-supporting activity other than primitive farming. In addition to the high rainfall the winters can be bitterly cold; in some years over a hundred days of frost have been recorded, and even October is not too early for it. Faced with conditions of this kind the native *morvandiaux* have tended to live in small communities containing only a few families, as though huddled together for protection. A traditional house consists of a single storey, often of one room, with hay and straw kept in the roof and providing a primitive but effective form of insulation. The granite from which they are made breaks too easily for neat building blocks to be cut and many houses appear rough and poorly finished. Once it was common for the roof to be thatched but now slates or even artificial tiles are more usual. Similarly, the most exposed walls of the house would once have been covered with strips of chestnut or slate but in recent years these traditional materials have been replaced by commercial ones and not always tastefully – official control over the refurbishment of old buildings appears not to have been as strict as it might be. Such harsh living conditions, here as in many similar areas, have almost inevitably caused local people to acquire the reputation of being mean, taciturn and even backward. There is a much quoted saying that *'Il ne vient du Morvan ni bonnes gens, ni bon vent'* ('Neither good people nor good wind come from the Morvan'), but if the second part has some truth in it the first has very little. Today about 30,000 people live in the Morvan, less than half of the number there were in the 1960s, and the population is diminishing further. For just over every two permanently occupied houses there is now one *résidence secondaire*, often owned, it must be said, by people whose family originates from the area. But among those who have remained, traditional Morvan hospitality is generous, and certainly out of the main tourist season a meal in a small restaurant or café (it is always worth asking even at the most modest-looking establishment what they might be able to provide) with a huge log fire blazing in an open hearth is an experience not to be missed. There is nothing exotic about *la cuisine morvandelle*, and the wine you are offered to accompany it will probably be a very ordinary and imported Côte du Rhone, but it is extraordinarily tasty. Much basic cooking is in the form of vegetable soups but the most celebrated dishes are constructed around ham. A large piece will normally have been cured in brine and a variety of herbs for a month or so. On removal from this mixture (known as the *saumure*) it is washed in *liqueur de prune* (further west, in the Charentes region, for example, this would be cognac) and then dried in wood ash. It can be eaten cold or hot, often with a sauce made from vinegar, chopped shallots, juniper berries, pepper and cream.

Chicken is also popular and a dish known as *le jau* – a bird less than a year old – cooked with small pieces of ham and onions in a sauce made from the bird's blood with a little vinegar is every bit as tasty as the better known and widely marketed *poulet de Bresse* from the area around Bourg across the Saône. Fish is plentiful (the pike, perch, trout and gudgeon attract over 50,000 hopeful fishermen every year) and pancakes (*grapiaux*) stuffed with ham pieces make a substantial snack. Goat cheeses, especially from Anost or Lormes, rival those of Provence though they are usually best eaten before they become too hard.

Access to this unique region, at least by car, is easiest by way of the principal road crossing from Château-Chinon to Autun, and there are plenty of smaller roads, many but not all in good condition, which allow you to penetrate the interior of the Morvan. Inevitably the car is the solution adopted by thousands, but the *parc* also attracts and caters for those who wish to explore on bicycle, horseback or on foot. A Tour du Morvan which takes in the six lakes has been established, and in part follows the Grande Randonnée 13 which itself runs from Vézelay to just west of Autun. The Tour is over 200 kilometres long and, while always following well-marked and well-maintained tracks, can be quite a strenuous undertaking. Most people choose to walk it in daily stages of 20–30 kilometres, and there are plenty of stopping places offering simple accommodation of youth-hostel quality. Information about this – or other walks – and about other facilities and indeed all aspects of life in the Morvan is provided by the helpful and enthusiastic staff of the Maison du Morvan which has been created at Saint-Brisson just north of the Lac des Settons. Also in the village is the important Musée de la Résistance which keeps alive the memory of the important contribution the area made to the struggle against Nazi occupation and, sadly, of the price that all too often had to be paid.

Traditionally the Morvan is divided into two parts: Le Bas Morvan to the north and Le Haut Morvan to the south. In fact there are rather four areas with distinct features: a northern part spreading south from Avallon, full of gentle valleys and rising to around 500 metres; a central one around the Lac des Settons, often up to 200 metres higher, with various viewpoints reached in the main by well-tended paths; a western strip with shallow hollows and *étangs*; and the dramatic south-eastern corner and the steep escarpment down to the valley of the Arroux and Autun.

If you come up the Morvan from the west and the vast expanses of the Nièvre, Château-Chinon is an ideal point for exploring in any direction. As we have already noted, the village enjoys the title and prestige of being the capital of the Morvan. Certainly its site and its history are impressive. It dominates a pass at 500 metres, and on the north side the land rises steeply to the point (at 609 metres) known as Le Calvaire where there are three plain crosses. Here traces have been found of a civilization, probably an Aedui settlement, dating from 200 BC. The village suffered mixed fortunes during the Middle Ages, being severely damaged during the wars of religion and in the struggles between France and Burgundy. By the seventeenth century, however, it was emerging as an important commercial centre with cattle sales and in particular a November log market at which the prices of wood were fixed, thereby determining the cost of domestic fuel in Paris. By the nineteenth century Château-Chinon was a thriving centre of over 3000 people, but inevitably as the log trade declined so it suffered too, and by the beginning of the twentieth century its population had halved. Since then tourism has helped in a revival, but the most influential factor has been Mitterrand's election in 1981 to the Presidency. In buildings which once formed part of the eighteenth-century convent of Sainte-Claire, a museum was established in 1988 (the Musée du Septennat) in which the gifts offered to Mitterrand in his capacity as head of the French state have been collected. They come from all parts of France as well as from every continent, but an especially interesting section is the one devoted to the offerings from France's African colonies. Mitterrand also allows gifts made to him personally to be displayed. This is a real cult museum, attracting thousands of visitors each year and providing the village with a substantial income. Thanks largely to this Château-Chinon has grown again, and with residential development in nearby hamlets and the appearance in the area called Les Gargouillats of some light industry in the 1960s, there is now an active population of over 3000.

Of the medieval fortifications, built by Louis XI after the defeat of the Burgundians, the only remains are the solid towers of the Porte Notre-Dame near the tourist information centre and on the main road to Autun (D978). Instead of leaving by this route, however, two others are prettier. On one, just to the north and before you rejoin the road at Arleuf, are the remains of a Gallo-Roman theatre. (The Tour du Morvan also passes through this point.) Built on a slope in the traditional semi-circular shape, it would have accommodated, according to archeologists, up to 700 spectators at both public meetings and theatrical performances, suggesting a thriving community. Continuing north, the road climbs over two sharp rises and then follows the contours of the hill north-west to the Lac de Pannecière. From the cluster of houses known as Les Brenets a network of paths spreads north, one of which leads to the memorial of the Resistance group known as Socrate.

The second route to follow from Château-Chinon is through Montignon with its squat, slate-roofed houses, and along the Yonne, which rises 15 kilometres further south in the shadow of Mont Préneley and near the hamlet of Anvers. Here again excavations have uncovered an area that was clearly a place of worship dating from at least 200 BC and almost certainly linked in some way with the important Gallo-Roman settlement at Bibracte just to the south. You are here on the very edge of the highest part of the Morvan and exploration on foot or on horseback is the most rewarding means of appreciating it. But there is a properly made, if narrow and tortuous, road which cuts through thick forest by way of Glux-en-Glenne and Saint-Prix to the Gorges de la Canche. A small dam has caused the river to broaden and stopping places on the road have been tastefully formed from which you have attractive views of it. It is possible to walk down and around the river at this point and, in a forest predominantly of pines, enjoy the relatively rare sight in this part of the Morvan of lime trees, maples and sycamores. Just near by as well is the modernized Refuge du Parc on the Grande Randonnée 13, a simple forest house, nearly 200 years old. From here a stiff climb up through the Forêt de Saint-Prix takes you to the summit of Haut-Folin and the very roof of the Morvan.

Directly south from here and only a couple of kilometres beyond the source of the Yonne is the most celebrated peak of the area, Mont Beuvray and the Oppidum de Bibracte. From a distance the approaches to Mont Beuvray appear deceptively gentle but once you are at the top, a vast platform, you realize that in fact the land falls away quite sharply through beech woods and that the site is ideal for any encampment or fortress. What is more, the local land contains deposits of iron ore, manganese and kaolin, for example, which in the distant past provided a sound basis on which to build an economy. Like the other peaks in the south-east corner of the Morvan, Beuvray is volcanic in origin, a fact indicated by the huge boulders and cracks in the rocky surface. One of these boulders, the Pierre de la Wivre (or *La Vouivre* as in the title of Marcel Aymé's strange novel), is said to cover the lair of a fabulous dragon guarding a vast hoard of treasure. Such tales are not uncommon in Burgundy or in Provence – La Chèvre d'Or near Les Baux in the Alpilles is a well-known example – and find their way into all kinds of mythological works, fiction and opera. According to one version the dragon appears, moving the stone and uncovering the treasure during the night of Christmas Eve; according to another, probably older pagan version, this happens on the winter solstice. Common to both versions is the belief that no-one attempting to steal some of the treasure has ever been known to return.

The wealth of the first major Aedui settlement at Bibracte (named after an ancient goddess of nature) was more modest, but the community which flourished from 200 BC was important and prosperous. For a long time they enjoyed good relations with the Romans, to whom they appealed in 58 BC for help in defending themselves against raiding Germanic bands from the east. But when Vercingetorix called for resistance against the occupying forces six years later they joined in the revolt and ensuing battles which Julius Caesar chronicles in his *Gallic Wars*. After his victory Caesar decided to settle in Bibracte, which he described as being the biggest and richest of the Aedui communities, but under the emperor Augustus the local Roman administrative headquarters moved to the town that is now Autun (Augustodunum), and Bibracte became steadily forgotten despite some occupation during the Middle Ages. In the nineteenth century first excavations of the site were undertaken principally by an amateur archeologist, Jacques-Gabriel Bulliot, and later by his nephew, but it was not until the 1980s that work was carried out in a systematic fashion and the ruins given special national status. Today the 135 hectares whose defences, now just a ridge, would have been 5 kilometres long have been carefully laid out and it is easy to appreciate the full extent of this ancient 'city' with its forges, temples, domestic buildings, mills and stockade for horses. Many of the objects which have been discovered, from richly enamelled jewels, pottery and money to pieces of harness and tools, have been placed in the national museum at Saint-Germain-en-Laye, but fortunately the Musée Rolin in Autun has some as well. Inevitably Mont Beauvray is popular with tourists and local people alike, and although a spacious car-park keeps vehicles well away from the main site, the presence of modern man in large numbers inevitably detracts from the air of mystery. The perfect time to be here is at night, preferably under a full winter's moon and when a storm is brewing. Then it is not only mysterious but frightening.

The journey from Bibracte to Autun is easier now than it was for the Romans 2000 years ago. Before making it, however, a visit should be paid to Saint-Honoré-les-Bains, just outside the south-western corner of the Morvan. Having discovered thermal springs in the area the Romans were here too; they called the town Aquae Nisincii. Benedictine monks buried the Roman remains in the tenth century and it was not until the middle of the nineteenth that the Marquis Théodore d'Espeuilles, having rediscovered the ancient installations, decided to develop a spa which was eventually opened to the public in 1860. Today over 7000 people come to Saint-Honoré each year, multiplying the stable population nearly tenfold. Over a million litres of water from three springs (La Garenne, La Crevasse and Les Romains) and at a temperature between 27 and 35 degrees centigrade are used to treat respiratory and bronchial problems in particular, and especially in children, and place the spa amongst the best known in France. As with many spa towns there is an air of slight seediness in Saint-Honoré, with its rows of hotels and houses, some neo-Gothic in style, others with half-timbering like

Normandy villas, others with turrets and pinnacles looking as though they came from a fairy-tale. The baths themselves are housed in a proud Second Empire building with some modern extensions, overlooking a fine expanse of parkland planted with oaks which slopes gently down to the west. Whether you decide to sample the waters or not, Saint-Honoré is distinctly different from anything else in the region and, if you have spent the day winding through the forest of the Morvan, makes a pleasant and restful place to stop for refreshment.

From Saint-Honoré a minor road intertwines with the southern boundary of the *parc* through Larochemillay (where the Grande Randonnée 13 and the Tour du Morvan merge), Saint-Léger-sous-Beuvray and La Grande-Verrière. Together they offer a good illustration of the depopulation to have affected this region, with each village only properly coming alive during the summer months as the *résidences secondaires* are opened up, and on the last Sunday in October when Saint-Léger puts on its renowned chestnut fair – though even this is now predominantly a tourist attraction selling as many plastic toys, bottles of wine, bars of soap and local cheeses as chestnuts. Between Saint-Léger and La Grande-Verrière the road also follows the narrow valley of the Méchet and after about 3 kilometres both suddenly veer right as though being squeezed out on to the plain stretching east to Autun.

Autun

With a population of about 17,000, Autun at the end of the twentieth century is less than a quarter of the size it is claimed to have been at the height of its Gallo-Roman period. Founded thirty years after Lyon, Augustodunum developed quickly into an important administrative, legal and intellectual centre. For centuries it enjoyed this status despite being the target of inevitable aggressions from local tribes, the Germanic invasions and in the ninth century from the Saracens. One siege in particular in 269, which lasted for about a year, did considerable damage and much of the town had to be rebuilt. With difficult communications Autun declined both in size and importance after the collapse of the Roman Empire, but still remained a centre of learning and artistic activity. With incorporation into Burgundy in the tenth century and the development of religious life around the cathedral two centuries later, the town experienced a steady if mild revival. This continued until the eighteenth century and is reflected in the high proportion of fine town houses and public buildings, rivalling those to be found in Auxerre. The Revolution took its toll — though fortunately the cathedral was spared — and with the administrative reorganization of France under Napoleon Autun lost its former status. Not to be outdone, it turned its attention to industry seriously for the first time and began to exploit the local schist deposits to make oil — an activity which would only be forced to shut down in the 1950s in the face of competition from America. A furniture industry was also created and the 'fair' in Autun during the last week of August is probably the major furniture exhibition in France other than the one held in Paris. More recently still textiles have been added to the small industrial output of Autun, but increasingly the town relies on tourism and cultural activities such as the celebrated choral festival in July, the Musique en Morvan, for its income.

From its earliest years Autun has relatively few architectural remains. The most extensive are those of the Roman theatre on the eastern edge of the town, where 12,000 spectators could be accommodated. Serious excavation work was begun in the 1930s but much remains to be done, and even though a great deal of the original stone has been appropriated over the centuries for building there is no doubt that with time and money a site could be uncovered which might rival parts of the Roman remains in Lyon. The other two major witnesses to the Roman presence are the Porte Saint-André, less than a kilometre north of the theatre, and the Porte d'Arroux on the other side of the town and overlooking the river. These are two of the original four entrances through the 6 kilometres of the town's fortifications, and while considerably restored they still retain their two large arches for the passage of carts and horses and two small ones for pedestrians. When Stendhal visited Autun in the early nineteenth century he recorded in his diary that after a surfeit of Gothic churches the gates made him feel as though he were back in Italy. He also commented on the only other significant piece of Roman building to survive today, the so-called Temple de Janus. 'The peasant who owns the field is complaining that this odd building attracts people who cause damage and I think he will soon get permission to knock it down.' Fortunately he appears not to have bothered or to have had permission refused, and the two walls (hence probably the name Janus, given to it in the sixteenth century) of what is now thought to have been an advance look-out post rather than a religious building remain. During the dry conditions in 1976 aerial photographs of Autun revealed that it formed part of an important collection of buildings including another amphitheatre and possibly a spa. These too remain to be properly excavated.

Of the original walls quite a lot remains, the best section being on the west side of the city flanked by the Boulevards des Resistants and MacMahon, leading to the southern tip of Autun, its highest point and known as the *ville haute*. As the town shrank after the Roman decline this became the new centre, clustered around the cathedral. To appreciate its position and organization it is best to climb up the wooded slopes of either of the two hills just to the south of the town, to the stark Croix de la Résistance or to the intriguing Pierre de Couhard, a curious stone like a massive termites' nest, now known to have been either a place of burial or a cenotaph. From either of these high points you can see how the cathedral of Saint-Lazare dominates the foreground and how the rest of Autun spreads north like an open fan. A more detailed impression of the same perspective is had from the parapet at the base of the spire of the cathedral itself.

Until the eighteenth century Saint-Lazare was surrounded by small churches and dependent chapels which, with their towers and spires, must have caused Autun to rival Nevers in appearance. A cathedral church has been on this site since the twelfth century when the first edifice was built to house the remains of Lazarus, which had hitherto been in the older church of Saint-Nazaire. After the completion of Saint-Lazare around 1146 the two churches shared activities; Saint-Lazare was used in the winter, Saint-Nazaire in the summer. The latter was eventually demolished in the eighteenth century. Although the ground plan and some of the original Romanesque features of the church can still be seen today, it has undergone considerable restoration. The first tower was destroyed by lightning in 1469 and the present bigger octagonal one is the work of one of Autun's great benefactors, Jean Rolin (the son of Nicolas who was responsible, of course, for the Hospices de Beaune). This new steeple is more Gothic in style than the first, as are the slightly pointed arches and vaults which no longer have that perfect curve which you find at Tournus or Vézelay, for example. The side chapels were added a hundred years later and the west towers rebuilt in the nineteenth century.

The internationally famous feature of the outside of the cathedral is the tympanum in the south-west porch depicting the Last Judgement. Its survival is due to chance. In 1766 the local priests, who disliked it, covered it with a screed of plaster with the result that they almost certainly saved it from destruction at the time of the Revolution. In 1837 it was rediscovered except for Christ's head which was missing and was not found and identified until 1948. The tympanum is recognized as being by the master mason Gislebert, who lived and worked in Autun for about twenty years from 1125. On the edge of the lintel, just beneath Christ's feet, is inscribed 'Gislebertus hoc fecit'. The figures and symbols are those which we find, for example, in the tympanum of Vézelay, where it is believed Gislebert studied for a while, and in Van der Weyden's painting in Beaune. Christ occupies the central panel. To his right are the blessed and good, including the apostles, with Saint Peter carrying his key over his shoulder and supervising entry into heaven for the lucky ones. The damned – including a miser, a drunkard, a woman representing lust with her breasts being eaten by a snake and another unfortunate sinner already in the grip of a devil's claws – know what is in store for them. Saint Michael is the master of ceremonies. Inside Saint-Lazare the work of Gislebert and his pupils is also much in evidence in the carved capitals. Quite a few of the originals were replaced in the nineteenth century when repair and strengthening work was being carried out, and a dozen of them are now on display in the chapter house, reached by a stairway just to the south of the choir. Others were left *in situ*, and a lighting system enables you to study them in reasonable detail. Guide books available in the church interpret the medieval symbolism for you just as they describe the tympanum in detail, but whatever the stories behind them, what catches the eye is the liveliness and realism of the work of someone traditionally held to be a rather sober artist. The stoning of Saint Stephen just by the pulpit, the baptism of Saint Paul — in a barrel — almost opposite on the third column from the main door, are full of life. In the chapter house the touching depiction of the three wise men sharing a narrow bed after they have lost sight of the star is offset by the brutality of Cain dying, having been shot through the throat by an arrow, or of Judas, hanging, with the rope being pulled over the branch of a tree by a pair of devils.

More of Gislebert's work can be admired in the Musée Rolin north of Saint-Lazare in the Rue des Bancs, notably the famous carving of Eve ('*Eve couchée*'), once part of the lintel beneath the tympanum. This depicts Eve in the crucial act of picking the apple. She is nude, lying in or crawling through foliage and with her eyes open, and her right hand cupped around her mouth could be imagined calling to Adam. The sexuality is powerful. Throughout the rest of this remarkable museum (certainly among the best in Burgundy) is a collection much of which has been gathered together and provided by the local historical and archeological society, the Société Éduenne. As we might expect, the Gallo-Roman and medieval worlds dominate. Tombs, mosaics, domestic equipment, agricultural tools, religious effigies, paintings and statues proliferate. There is also a collection of paintings from the sixteenth to the early twentieth centuries with some rather dull local work depicting interiors and landscapes which do not suggest that the 'Autun school', as it is somewhat pretentiously called, has a great deal to offer. In general, however, the display is good and many individual items deserve close attention, but after '*Eve couchée*' none is better to my mind than the small polychrome stone statue of the Virgin holding the infant Jesus tightly wrapped in swaddling. There is nothing premonitory or grand about this; it is utterly tender, domestic and private.

Although in the late twentieth century Autun has a rather uncertain air about it, outside the tourist season at least, the former medieval ease and importance of this southern tip of the town is still easy to appreciate. In the tiny passage of the Jeu-de-Paume, a reminder that a court for this early version of tennis was somewhere here, is possibly the finest town house of all Autun. Medieval in origin, it was substantially renovated in the eighteenth century and for a while belonged to the Schneider family. The narrow Rue Notre-Dame has houses which were once made available for those connected with the cathedral. In the Rue Dufraigne you find some typical timbered houses, to be compared with similar ones further north in Auxerre or Joigny, and where this street joins the Rue de Faubourg-Saint-Blaise was the site of one of the original medieval gates, La Poste Matheron. Few towns in Burgundy offer such a marked contrast between their *quartier mediéval* and more recent, classical buildings than Autun. Inevitably much of the *ville haute* has been prettified for tourists but it is still possible, particularly in mid winter, to wander through these streets, meet virtually no-one, hear only the sounds of church bells and imagine not only what life here was like four or five hundred years ago but also be oblivious of the wider streets and squares which characterize much of the modern *ville basse*.

The focal point of the lower part of Autun is the Champs de Mars. On its south-west side is the Lycée Bonaparte, originally a Jesuit college begun early in the eighteenth century but owing its present name to the fact that Napoleon Bonaparte and his two brothers Joseph and Lucien were pupils here for a while in the 1780s. It has a particularly splendid wrought-iron and gilded main gate and railings bearing the crest of Louis XVI. I personally find the *lycée*, like much of this part of Autun, rather too austere, though there are some fine examples of eighteenth-century town houses with balconies and courtyards in the streets just off the square (Rues Saint-Saulge and de l'Arquebuse, for example) which are every bit as grand as those to the south of the Place de la République in Dijon. A number of features do catch the eye, however. One is a series of outside stairways which are a reminder of the difficulties posed by housing demand in the second half of the eighteenth century. In the Rue Chauchien, south of the Champ de Mars, for example, there are several. Demand was such that there was increasingly less space available to build the traditional town residence with courtyard and garden, and houses were constructed directly on the street. The outside stairs, usually wooden and often double, allowed people living in the upper floors to have their own private entrance, rather like modern maisonettes.

Another interesting feature in this area is a covered passage between the Rue des Cordiers and the Rue Demetz. Originally an open alleyway lined with wooden shops, it was covered and developed in the mid nineteenth century and paid for by public subscription – a way of raising finance which made it unique in France. So splendid was it that the local paper, the *Echo de Saône-et-Loire*, compared it to similar passages in Lyon. Gradually it fell into disrepair, but in the 1970s it was fully restored and must now be as elegant as the citizens of Autun could have hoped. It has shops on the ground floor and on a gallery running the full length of the arcade on either side, to which there is access by a modest but not inelegant stairway. The pillars supporting the gallery have mock-Corinthian capitals, and the balustrade is richly carved. It is now a very fashionable (if expensive) place to shop, and a popular meeting place. The only other arcade of this kind in Burgundy is the Passage Manifacier in Auxerre, which dates from about the same time and has also been restored in recent years.

North of Autun the roads fan out in various directions. To re-enter the Morvan the most attractive route is to go back towards Château-Chinon and then branch north to Cussy-en-Morvan, either along the valley of the Ternin to Sommant, with its mill, pigeon-tower and cluster of fortified houses, or along the narrower valley of the Celle. In the opposite direction, however, the opportunity should not be missed to visit Sully, just 20 kilometres east of Autun, where what some consider to be the most elegant château in Burgundy is to be found. In a much quoted phrase Madame de Sévigné called it the 'Fontainebleau of Burgundy'. Some kind of fortified dwelling was here in the thirteenth century but most of the present pale stone building (which is not open to the public) dates from the very end of the fifteenth. As you approach it along a well-kept drive between stable blocks, edged with neatly trimmed box hedges, you notice at once the massive square towers at an angle on each corner. While these and other parts of the façade have been altered over the years, notably in the eighteenth century by the Morey family, who added a huge terrace and a monumental stairway on the north side, the château still manages to appear to be a unified whole. When this staircase was built it probably led to an empty moat, which for several decades was used for rearing wild animals. Since the 1890s it has been filled with water from the Drée and the reflection is most effective. After the Morey family, the château passed into the possession of the staunch royalists the Mac-Mahon, who own it today. Several members of the family have made important contributions to French history, not least Patrice, who after a distinguished career in Algeria and Italy was President of the Third Republic between 1873 and 1879. He was also responsible for the brutal suppression of the Commune in Paris in 1870. But it is around his grandmother Charlotte that a local legend developed. It is said that at the time of the Revolution she was accused of sending money to her sons who had fled France. Because of her advanced age it was decided she should be allowed to die naturally before the château was requisitioned by the state. She did eventually die in 1798 but her death was kept secret. Her servants are said to have preserved her body in a trough of alcohol, only taking it out and putting it in her bed every time the château was inspected. In this way Sully was saved from being taken over by the officials of the new Republic!

From Cussy-en-Morvan or Anost you are once again in a position of being able to explore the whole central area of the Morvan. Barely 5 kilometres to the north is the attractive *village perché* of Ménessaire (in fact administratively part of the Côte d'Or *département*), and beyond is the series of high points (around 670 metres) known as the Monts de Moux, which are linked by the Tour du Morvan. Moux itself sits on the slopes of the hills to which it has given its name. Roman in origin, it now depends amost entirely on tourism for its livelihood and the road west to the Lac des Settons is often packed with cars ands cyclists during the summer months. Unless your preferred forms of relaxation at this time express themselves in a taste for water-sports, crowded beaches, fast food and pop music, the lake is to be avoided. But a visit out of season is not without interest. For a decade now the authorities have carefully scrutinized applications for new buildings, but the range of dwellings, especially along the north-eastern side, from simple huts to substantial brick-built villas and ranches, are a legacy from the 1960s when people from Autun in particular could buy pockets of land and develop them as they wished. During the years following the lake's centenary in 1959 much effort was also expended in developing a system of forest paths, picnic areas, car-parks, camp sites and holiday villages, to accommodate and cater for the swelling numbers of tourists. It has to be acknowledged that the whole scheme has been an intelligent adaptation of a facility whose original purpose has long disappeared, and that economically it has been invaluable. But as increasing numbers of people turn inland for their holidays and recreation, away from the beaches which the media each summer delight in presenting as overcrowded and polluted, new problems will be created. The wear and tear on the banks of the lake and immediate surrounding areas are evident, and however careful the authorities are the ecological balance is bound to be upset. In this respect the much more recent (1949) Lac de Pannesière provides an interesting comparison. The fact that it is drained most years has discouraged extensive development of water-sports and lakeside building and, so far at least, has allowed much of it to maintain a more natural appearance, though the hydro-electric plant at its northern point is hardly notable for its charm, despite the magnificent views from the top of the dam. Both lakes are best visited either when it is very cold or when it is raining: you are then likely to be alone.

From Moux the main road heads north through Alligny-en-Morvan following the steep-sided valley of the Ternin to Saulieu. A smaller one to the east passes through Marnay and then across a more gentle countryside to Pierre-Ecrite. Here in the tiny village square, leaning against a lime tree, is a worn Gallo-Roman stone slab (from which the village takes its name) bearing traces of a carving which shows five people in the top section and three smaller in the lower. There is no agreement as to its significance, but given that one person to the left appears to be standing behind a table or counter it seems to me not unlike the slabs depicting the butcher and wine-seller in Dijon. Also in the village is the inn (designated by a plaque) where Napoleon stayed on his way north to Paris in 1815. The route he took led directly then, as it does today, to Saulieu.

Saulieu
Set on the very eastern edge of the Morvan, Saulieu has for centuries been a meeting point between the hills to the west and the plains of the Auxois to the north-east, as well as a

staging post on the main road, originally the Via Agrippa, between Autun and Avallon. From the Middle Ages its importance as a commercial centre grew rapidly, with wine, wood, hemp, grain, fish and tiles all being central to its activities up to the mid nineteenth century, and reflected in the names of several of the streets. The town also has more fairs than any other in Burgundy. But here as elsewhere the improvements in the road system and the arrival of the railway in 1882 served to take people away rather than bring them to Saulieu, and its population declined substantially. In the period between the two World Wars the town enjoyed a growing reputation as a gastronomic centre, but this too was undermined by the construction of the motorway (A6) which enabled tourists and Parisians in particular to pursue their journey further south before having to consider refreshment. And yet Saulieu has not surrendered. The creation of the Parc Régional has unquestionably increased tourist trade, but the local council has also worked hard to promote the town's image and a new exhibition centre built on the outskirts is busy all the year round.

The centre of Saulieu is dominated by the twelfth-century basilica church of Saint-Andoche, built on the site of an abbey thought by some to have been there five centuries earlier. Frequently damaged both by extremes of weather and by human hand, the church has been much restored, but fortunately the nave and even more importantly the capitals, which rank as highly in medieval ecclesiastical art as does Gislebert's work in Saint-Lazare, survive. The subjects are varied – leaf designs, animals, birds and scenes from the New Testament – but the artist is unknown. A link of some kind between the two men seems likely, and while Saulieu's master sculptor is generally thought to have been less gifted than Gislebert, the judgement is to my mind a harsh one. Certainly art historians are correct in pointing out that Judas' suicide (third pillar) lacks the violence of the sculpture of the same subject in Autun, but the cock-fight (fourth pillar) or the dancing goats (fifth pillar) display a realism that is every bit as impressive. And the mixture of fear and astonishment on the faces of Balaam and his ass when challenged by an angel bearing a sword is hardly matched anywhere by Gislebert or indeed by the masons of Vézelay. For these alone Saulieu is worth a detour and an hour of anybody's time. And once you have finished, pay a visit to the Côte d'Or hotel-restaurant, which will remind you – at a price – of Saulieu's other reputation, and where you will be following in the footsteps of Philippe Pétain and Charles de Gaulle, who dined here when its legendary chef was Alexandre Dumaine.

The same combination of ecclesiastical architecture and gastronomic delights is also to be found 50 kilometres to the northwest at Vézelay. The N6 leads swiftly to Avallon, but any of the smaller roads just to the south take you through one of the most mysterious parts of the Morvan, around Quarré-les-Tombes. The village, which is rather dull, owes its name to a collection of stone sarcophagi which lie around the local church of Saint-Georges. No-one knows why they are there or where they come from. Dating has shown that they are from the late seventh or early eighth centuries, but whether they are the remains of a sanctuary, have been associated with some cult around Saint George or, more prosaically, are simply what remains of some Merovingian supplier's goods is uncertain. But this is an area rich in remains of the distant past and mysterious stones and grottoes.

One of these, deep in the forest of pines and beech trees to the east of Quarré, is the Pierre-qui-Vire, 'the stone which turns'. Roads leading here seem to go on for ever, and with quite a lot of surface water the atmosphere is frequently damp and misty. The stone is a massive, flat block of granite, the origins and purpose of which are simply not known. A theory that it was a burial chamber has long been discredited, but a legend that it was a place of worship for a pagan cult and turned at various times of the year still survives. While the truth is that it is probably a natural phenomenon, the result of erosion by wind and rain, it is nonetheless unusual and, as though to counteract any potential pagan forces which might have been contained in it, the founder of the Benedictine monastery here in the mid nineteenth century, Jean-Baptiste Muard, had a statue of the Virgin Mary put on top of it.

When it was inaugurated in 1850 the community had only five monks; within twenty years this number had grown tenfold, and today there are just over a hundred. The monastery walls and buildings are constructed from rough-hewn blocks of local stone, though brick has been used in the church roof for the vaulting. Visits are not permitted, other than to the church during certain services, to a shop and to an exhibition room (as at Cîteaux) where a video display describes community life. The main door, in local oak and surrounded by a modern carving of Christ in majesty with Mary, Moses, Abel and Saint Peter, has a central pillar in the form of a rather sad Benedictine monk holding his staff and pointing upwards to the figure of Christ. At the bottom and to the left of the door is a greeting to pilgrims and vagabonds, and the monks are well known for the hospitality they offer to people who, for whatever reason, have nowhere else to go. The abbey also welcomes those who wish to spend a week in retreat here, and encouragement is given to participate as fully as possible in community life. The monks work a nearby farm at L'Huis-Benoît, where they have been trying for some years to develop farming methods suitable for the local terrain and climate. One result of this is an excellent range of cheeses which are much sought after locally. Farming has not always been easy, however. In 1969 the monks' herd had to be entirely replaced after the cows had become poisoned by chemical sprays and fertilizers. Recovery was costly and slow, but by the 1980s milk yields had improved dramatically on earlier ones. The cheese, now organically made, is sold either in a small size under the abbey's name or in a larger cutting version known as Le Trinquelin. The sales now provide half the abbey's income. The monks also have a pottery and, since 1948, a studio for works of sacred art. With an eye to the commercial potential of such activities, they have also opened their own printing works and, with a collection known as the Zodiaque press, specialize in books devoted to Romanesque art and architecture. The reasons for this specialization are quite clear: Romanesque capitals and tympanums depict the true presence of Christ in an unsentimental and direct fashion. Saint Bernard would have thoroughly approved.

From the Lac de Saint-Agnan the valleys of the Trinquelin or of the Cousin (the two are confused) can be followed north to Saint-Léger-Vauban. The village itself, while attractive enough, has nothing of particular architectural interest, but it is renowned as being the birthplace of Sébastien le Prestre, who was promoted in 1703 to the highest military rank of *maréchal de France* under Louis XIV for his skills as an engineer and his contributions to the defences of France throughout the country, from Lille in the north to Toulon on the Mediterranean coast. After the battle of Maastricht in 1673 he had already been rewarded by the king with the huge sum of 80,000 *livres*, which had enabled him to buy the land of Vauban (from which he then took his title) and the château of Bazoches to the south of Vézelay, where his body is buried. (In 1808 Napoleon had his heart interred in Les Invalides in Paris.) Vauban's links with Saint-Léger are commemorated by a bronze statue of him clutching plans in one hand and pointing authoritatively with the other, and by an exhibition housed in a disused school known as 'La Maison de Vauban', but his real presence is witnessed on a much grander scale at Bazoches where the château has been restored largely to the state it was in when he lived there. The stables and outbuildings, enlarged so as to be able to cope with his many commissions, can be visited, as can his study and private chapel or the offices for his engineers and draughtsmen. Such was the activity in and around Bazoches that it must have been a constant source of speculation for the local population.

Portraits of Vauban show him to be kind but firm and thoughtful, and somehow not quite like the man whose life was devoted to military exploits, albeit of a defensive nature. This concern for others was what caused him eventually in 1696 to propose a new taxation system whereby each person would pay according to his wealth, measured by the land he owned – in other words, a system which would considerably improve the lot of the poor people whom he saw all around him in the Morvan. But it was considered to be revolutionary and he lost royal favour as a result. Nonetheless he retained his possessions, and while, because of problems of succession, the château passed to other hands it is with him that it is regularly associated and he continues to be remembered with esteem and affection by local people.

North of Saint-Léger-Vauban and Quarré, the land slopes down across a number of shallow valleys crossed by the meandering Cousin, in which woodland gives way to pasture towards Avallon. Villages like Saint-Brancher, Villiers-Nonains or Marrault, with their neat, cream-coloured stone houses and occasional pigeon lofts or dovecotes roofed with local *lauzes*, bear witness to a prosperous past, but more often than not owe their present well-being to those Parisians whose weekday flats and offices are less than two hours' drive away. At the same time there is much intensive arable and cattle farming here and the tract of land which sweeps round north-west to merge with the Auxerrois has an atmosphere of ease and of 'mellow fruitfulness' which achieves a distinct serenity just a dozen kilometres to the west at Vézelay.

Avallon

The final stage of the southern approach to Avallon is across the steep valley of the Cousin, which runs east–west here and marks a clean break with the foothills of the Morvan. On a spur of rock on the Via Agrippa, Aballo, as it was originally called, enjoyed a strategic importance, but as a result was also the target for attacks from the Saracens in the eighth century and from the Normans a hundred years later. Worse was to come. Early in the eleventh century the king of France laid siege to the town and after three months, if tradition is correct, massacred all but 300 of its citizens. Thereafter, despite other wars and a number of plagues, Avallon gradually emerged as an important trading centre. Today its population of around 10,000 is twice what it was fifty years ago and is increased substantially at weekends and during holiday periods. But Avallon does not rely solely on tourists and second homes. In the northern outskirts, crossed by the N6, some light industry has developed and the area is generally one that has been carefully investigated by businesses wishing to move away from the Paris area and yet remain within reasonable proximity. Fortunately this development has not encroached on the older part of the town, which has kept its fortifications almost completely intact. Now a Tour des Remparts by way of well-kept paths, grassy banks and terraced gardens lined with plane and lime trees enables you to do a complete circuit of the medieval centre (in about an hour) or provides you with access at several points. Inside the walls the main axis is the cobbled Rue Bocquillot, now a pedestrian area, which links the principal buildings of interest. Towards the northern end of the street and forming an arch over it is the fifteenth-century Tour de l'Horloge, on the site of the gateway of the earlier château which covered most of the southern tip of the town; parts of it can still be glimpsed incorporated into some of the nearby houses. This is also where the first Roman encampment had been. For many years after the disappearance of the rest of the château the tower served as a lookout post, and from its belfry there are fine views to be had, especially of Vézelay and of the Morvan as it rises to the south. Next door to the tower is the seventeenth-century Couvent des Ursulines, and 100 metres further down on the opposite side of the road the former salt store, itself in a building which once housed the wine presses of the eleventh-century collegiate church of Saint-Lazare.

Of all Avallon's buildings, Saint-Lazare is by far the most interesting, though perhaps less exciting than some commentators and the Avallonnais themselves would have you believe. A church was here as early as the fourth century but it was not until seven centuries later that relics, supposedly of the saint, caused Avallon to become a place of pilgrimage, and the church was substantially rebuilt to accommodate the thousands who are said to have flocked here. Of the early building little remains intact. The most serious damage was done in 1633 when the north tower collapsed, destroying the left-hand doorway (where the present tower now is) and disrupting what would have been a group of three decorated Romanesque entrances unique in Burgundy and, it is thought, in France. Erosion and human damage have taken their toll of the remaining ones, as well; in particular the central figure of Christ has disappeared from the tympanum over the main door. But there are sufficient traces of decoration – signs of the Zodiac, angels, designs of leaves and vines, Old Testament figures or the Adoration, for example – for us to appreciate how splendid it must once have been. As you go into the church you are immediately struck by the fact that the floor of the nave is considerably lower than it is in the entrance; as the building follows the slope of the land, the apse is even more so. There is in fact an overall drop of about 3 metres. Being not very well lit, the interior also seems rather sombre and austere, but there are some interesting polychrome wooden statues of Christ, the Virgin Mary, the saints Peter, John and Julian and of the Annunciation. The best and most natural group of all in my view, however, is of Mary being taught to read by her mother Saint Anne – yet another example of the medieval Burgundian view of Christ's mother as a normal young woman.

When you leave the church it is worth exploring some of the nearby narrow streets in order to see how the houses have been modified over the years. Some remain still in need of very considerable restoration (and in the early 1990s the demand for *résidences secondaires*, even in a small town like Avallon, appears to have lessened); others have benefited from careful and intelligent work and are a credit to their owners who, more likely than not, will not be native. For all that it is undoubtedly attractive to many, I have to confess that I find Avallon in general somewhat pretentious and its citizens self-satisfied. I once had the misfortune to break down here. The good ladies of whom I asked information were concerned only that I had stopped where parking was not allowed, the *garagiste* was clearly unwilling to show any interest in my car for at least two days, and the manager of the hotel where I tried to stay admitted to having a room available only when pressed. Nowhere else in Burgundy have I encountered indifference to this degree.

Having left Avallon you eventually cross the valley of the Cousin at Pontaubert, where it was first bridged in 840. On the right a road follows the river to Vault-de-Lugny where, just south of the village, the château has been turned into a luxury hotel, but even if you cannot afford its prices its massive original thirteenth-century keep and the rather elegant moat are well worth seeing. In the village itself the church has an unusual sixteenth-century fresco above the bays in the nave and round the choir, with thirteen scenes depicting Christ's Passion. There are traces too of another painting on the west wall in which all the people appear to be black. The church at Pontaubert is also worth visiting. Three hundred years older than Saint-Germain in Vault-de-Lugny, and built by the Knights of Saint John from local granite, its vaulting nicely anticipates that in La Madeleine at Vézelay.

From Pontaubert, as indeed from miles around in all directions, the '*colline inspirée*', to use the poet Maurice Druon's celebrated phrase, draws the modern visitor as it did the medieval pilgrims who flocked there in their tens of thousands, either to worship at the shrine of Mary Magdalene or to continue on their way to Compostela. If time allows it is worth looping south, however, from the main road to follow a much smaller, but pretty route through Tharoiseau (a meeting place for pilgrims), Ménades and past the Fontaines Salées. These remains of thermal baths from Gallo-Roman times are some of the finest in France, and excavations have revealed evidence of a much older civilization still. Long wooden tubs or wells made of oak and estimated to be 3000 years old have been found, and while probably used in the exploitation of the curative properties of the salt water springs are thought also to be relics of a pagan cult. These tubs and some more recent (1000 BC) funerary jars can be seen in the archeological museum next door to the church of Notre-Dame in Saint-Père-sous-Vézelay. It is worth retaining a mental picture of the interior of this delicate, brightly lit church built from pale sandstone when you are eventually confronted by the splendours of La Madeleine.

Vézelay

It was in Saint-Père that the community which would eventually dominate the life of Vézelay was founded in 858. Within thirty years, however, the Normans had ransacked the monastery and the monks had taken refuge on the nearby hill where for centuries there had been Celtic camps and forts. In the tenth century a first church dedicated to Mary Magdalene was built, her relics having been brought here from Provence in order, so it was said – and the Pope authenticated the story – to save them from the marauding Saracens. A massive fire caused serious damage – and over a thousand deaths – in 1120 and much of the church had to be rebuilt; and further structural damage occurred over the next century. But Vézelay had become a major site on the map of Christian Europe, visited by Thomas Becket in 1166, in exile from Canterbury, and above all by Bernard, who twenty years earlier had preached the second crusade from the spot now marked by the Church of Sainte-Croix. At this time Vézelay supported a population of around 15,000 and attracted many times that number in the course of a year. (Today there are about 500 inhabitants, of whom a quarter at least are elderly, though it is estimated that the village receives more than half a million visitors a year!) But just over a century later disaster struck. In 1279 the sacred relics were declared to be fake and it was now claimed that Mary Magdalene's remains had in fact never strayed from the crypt of Saint-Maximin in Provence. Almost at once the village began to go into an eclipse which would last for nearly six centuries. Natural decay, plundering and official selling of the abbey church and buildings led Prosper Mérimée, who arrived here in 1814 in his capacity as Inspector of Historic Buildings, to write that the church was in a pitiful state, and 21 years later that there was no single part of it which was not in need of instant restoration. Responsibility for the task was given to the young architect Viollet-le-Duc in 1840. His work has not always been appreciated by everybody, but there can be no doubt that only by extensive restorative work could one of the greatest examples of Romanesque architecture in France be saved.

As at Autun, the amount of literature available charting and interpreting the various features of La Madeleine is so extensive that any attempt to consider the church and its ornamentation in any detail here would be completely inadequate. I am not alone in finding the outside relatively unattractive. The west façade lacks balance, the central window in particular, ornamented with statues of six saints, seems too heavy, and the single south tower (once topped with a wooden spire) pulls the whole edifice sideways. Once inside, however, things change. Above the central doorway of the narthex leading to the nave and supported on a central pillar bearing the figure of John the Baptist is the great tympanum depicting Christ bestowing on his apostles the gift (and duty) of spreading the word of God. Surrounding this central drama are figures representing the various nations to be addressed, some half animal in form, others almost deformed like pygmies or a group of people with big ears. But none are held in ridicule or contempt.

The narthex was, of course, a kind of ante-chamber to the church proper, in which worshippers could draw breath and consider the gravity of their next step. Even without such spiritual considerations, the fact that the narthex at Vézelay is poorly lit means that beyond the nave door, especially when the sun floods in from the east end, the body of the church seems alive. The effect is enhanced by the stone. The great round arches of the nave have alternate blocks of brown and cream, giving the church an almost Moorish appearance, as one of Vézelay's celebrated visitors, the novelist Marcel Proust, observed. Elsewhere the limestone has tints of pink, grey and even pale green, before giving way to the blinding white of the choir. And, whether the result of accident or careful design, there is another remarkable feature concerning the lighting in this church. At the summer solstice (and the feast of John the Baptist is 24 June) the rays of the midday sun produce thirteen circles of light precisely along the centre of the floor of the nave, as though marking a path leading from the narthex to the choir and altar, from darkness to light. If to this you add the symbolism which experts have attributed to the numbers of distribution of pillars in the choir (groups of twelve or of eleven – twelve apostles minus Judas – or of three and multiples thereof), the whole church begins to resonate with a spiritual significance that is almost uncanny.

This for me is the most striking feature of the church, though opportunities to be able to contemplate it alone, undisturbed by groups of guide-consulting, whispering tourists are unfortunately all too rare. For most people La Madeleine's principal attraction is its sculptures – the tympanum in the narthex and the capitals. The latter are certainly remarkable. In the nave all but six are original; some are carved with traditional designs of leaves and flowers, others depict fabulous beasts and birds, others again contain scenes from the Bible and from saints' lives or illustrate moral lessons. What is remarkable is that none describes directly any feature of Christ's life and, what is perhaps even more surprising, only one, in the narthex, illustrates the patron saint's. The capitals are thought to be the work of a single school of masons under the guidance of Pierre de Montboissier, who may or may not have known Gislebert who was responsible for those at Autun. There has always been debate about the respective qualities of the two collections but while many experts find those by Gislebert to be more lively or 'real', there seems to me to be little to choose between them, any more than there is with those, fewer in number admittedly, at Saulieu. Some are unwittingly amusing: the one depicting the temptation shows a full-breasted, almost brazen Eve offering the apple to Adam who pushes it away with a look of distinctly superior self-righteousness; as Noah wields his axe to build the ark his wife peers anxiously at him through one of the vessel's windows. Some are violent – the vision of Saint Anthony, the depiction of lechery as a woman whose belly is being eaten by a serpent (the symbolism here is evident), or that of despair, a demon with flaming hair thrusting a sword through his body. The capital of Moses carrying the tablets bearing the word of God and returning to find his countrymen still worshipping the golden calf is full of drama and action, as is the one telling the story of Saint Eugenia as she bares her breast to prove her true sex, flanked by her frustrated accuser and her bewildered father (and judge). But of them all the most celebrated and intriguing is the one known as the '*moulin mystique*', on the fourth pillar on the right, which shows one man pouring grain into a grinder and another carefully collecting it as flour. The first man is Moses, the second Saint Paul; the grain is the word of God brought down by Moses from Mount Sinai and which by the actions of Christ – the grinder is driven by a wheel whose spokes are in the form of a cross – is turned into the message of the New Testament. On account of both style and subject matter this capital is thought to be the work of the mason responsible for the tympanum in the narthex. All these and many more threaten to make of La Madeleine as much a museum as a place of worship, and while this may be inevitable the church's primary function should not be forgotten.

If this is still just possible within the church itself, once you are outside the modern world of tourism takes over. This is not to say that the village's medieval past has been totally eclipsed – far from it. The medieval Porte Neuve with its towers and battlements still guards the northern entrance, and it is possible to visit town houses with their vast cellars opening on to the street and in which pilgrims by the thousand were provided with primitive accommodation. (One suspects that several hundred years ago, just as today, quite a lot of money would have been made from these visitors!) But inevitably the late twentieth century takes its toll. Souvenir shops, bakers selling mouth-watering *pâtisseries* and wine merchants offering a Vézelay vintage lie in wait, modern temptations of the flesh on the way to or from the spiritual summit of the village. Yet for all the incursions of the modern world Vézelay has retained its mystique. Writers and artists have been drawn here and have celebrated it in their works: Romain Rolland, Max-Pol Fouchet, Claudel, Proust, Picasso, Georges Bataille, Le Corbusier, Jules Roy. Some are buried in the peaceful cemetery just down the slope to the northeast of the church. And it is not difficult to see why this should be. The most popular photographs of Vézelay show the lower half of the hill shrouded in mist rising from the valley of the Cure with the church floating magically above. For believers and unbelievers alike the spirit of Vézelay — another example of *'la force tranquille'* — prevails. And there can be few better places from which to contemplate it than from Saint-Père and the converted mill, now one of the best restaurants in France. Here, in the Espérance, Marc Meneau will provide you with turbot cooked in meat juices, hot *foie gras* in lentils or ice cream flavoured with pepper, and will offer you a local wine from vines which he has been largely responsible for replanting. None of this is cheap but the spiritual succour it provides after a long day's sightseeing is welcome.

Index

Aedui, 141, 154, 156
Alésia, 47–8
Aloxe-Corton, 61, 79, 85, 92
Ancy-le-Franc, 45, 134
Archéodrome (historical and pleasure park), 94–5
Autun, 5, 6, 25, 37, 56, 88, 89, 153, 154, 155, 156, 157, 158–64, 165, 167, 175, 176
Auxerre, 3, 14, 17, 18, 20, 31, 32–8, 50, 140, 141, 142, 159, 163, 164
Auxey-Duresses, 2
Avallon, 19, 153, 171–3
Azé, 109, 112

Bacon, Francis, 68
Bard, Joseph, 98
Bazoches, 128
Becket, Thomas, 14, 174
Beaune, 1, 5, 10, 26, 41, 48, 76, 84, 85, 86–92, 130, 161
   Hospices, 41
   Hôtel-Dieu, 89–91, 92, 108
   wine auctions, 84, 92
Bérégovoy, Pierre, 141
Bernard, Saint, 7–8, 14, 113, 174
Bertranges, Forêt de, 129, 134, 138–9
Berzé-le-Chatel, 119, 120
Berzé-la-Ville, 119–20

Bibracte, 155, 156–7
Bléneau, 26–7
Brancion, 102, 103–4, 109
Brosse, Claude, 101
Buffon, Comte de, 46
Bulliot, Jacques-Gabriel, 157

Canals, 6, 24, 54
   du Centre, 100, 115, 121, 123
   du Nivernais, 129, 135, 144, 147
   Latéral de la Loire, 123, 127, 140, 144
cassis, liqueur de, 63–4
Chablis, 2, 33, 38–40, 136
Chagny, 76, 79, 93, 97
Chalon-sur-Saône, 2, 76, 95–7, 105, 109, 111, 115, 124, 138, 141
Chapaize, 109–10, 113
charcoal, 135, 139, 151
Charité-sur-Loire, La, 10, 113, 130, 137–8
Charolles, 120, 121–2
Chassagne-Montrachet, 1, 79
Château-Chinon, 127, 147, 150, 153, 154–5, 164
Châtillon, 25
Châtillon-sur-Seine, 26, 42, 43–4
cheese, 51–2, 153, 169

Cîteaux, Abbaye de, 7, 70, 76, 82–3, 100, 131
Clamecy, 130, 134–6
Cluny, 7, 82, 98, 102, 106, 109, 111, 113–15, 120, 137
Colette, 25, 30, 129
Conant, Kenneth, 114
Confrérie des Chevaliers de la Pochouse, 93
Confrérie des Chevaliers du Tastevin, 83
Cormatin, 110–11, 120
Cosne, 10, 127, 129, 131–3, 138, 140
Courtenay, 24
Cousin, Jean, 12, 18
Creusot, Le, 4, 124, 125–6

Decize, 129, 144–5
De Gaulle, Charles, 3, 168
Digoin, 95, 123–4, 127, 150
Dijon, 2, 3, 5, 6, 7, 8, 9, 26, 44, 50, 53–75, 76, 77, 79, 80, 84, 86, 92, 95, 124, 128, 130, 141, 142, 163, 166
    Chartreuse de Champmol, 60, 66, 73, 74–5
    Foire Gastronomique Internationale, 60–2
    Musée des Beaux Arts, 57, 59, 65–7
    mustard, 53, 62–3
    Notre-Dame, 67–9
    pain d'épice, 62
    Saint-Bénigne, 71–3
Donzy, 128, 133, 134, 136
Druyes-les-Belles-Fontaines, 30–1
Dumas, Alexandre, 62

Eliot, T.S., 40
Époisses, 50–2

faïence, 4, 121, 131, 138, 140, 143
Ferté-Loupière, 22
Fixin, 2, 78, 79, 81–2
Flavigny, 49
Fleurigny, 11–12
Fontenay, Abbaye de, 15, 42, 46–7, 50
food, 8–9, 32, 152–3, 178

Gamay, 2, 94

Gevrey-Chambertin, 79, 82
Givry, 1, 79, 97, 100
Glaber, Raoul, 71
Goujon, Jean, 20, 25
Granville, Pierre, 66
Gregory of Tours, 55, 105
Guérigny, 139

Joan of Arc, 33, 40, 58
Joigny, 18, 20–3, 163

Kir, Félix, 54, 64
kir, 64
Knights of St John, 11, 44, 85, 173

Lamartine, Alphonse de, 111, 116, 119
Larousse, Pierre, 31
Le Vau, François, 27–8
Lyon, 56, 86, 98, 100, 108, 110, 128

Machine, La, 145
Mâcon, 2, 3, 4, 5, 58, 95, 96, 98, 99, 115–18, 130
Malraux, André, 40
Mann, Thomas, 40
Marsannay, 79, 80
Mauriac, François, 40
Mercurey, 79, 97
Mérimée, Prosper, 137, 175
Meursault, 1, 2, 61, 79, 92, 93–4
Miller, Henry, 53, 62, 75
Mitterrand, François, 119, 127, 154
monasteries, 3, 15, 40, 46–7
    and wine, 76–7, 100, 131
Montargis, 4, 23–5, 122
Montbard, 43
Mont Beuvray, 150, 156–7
Montceau-les-Mines, 4, 42, 120, 124, 125
Morvan, Parc régional du, 2, 4, 5, 25, 72, 115, 121, 127, 129, 135, 145, 147, 149–58, 164–70
    lakes, 150–1, 153, 165–6
    living conditions, 151–2
Motte-Josserand, La, 128, 133, 134
mustard, 53, 62–3

Napoleon I, 11, 81–2, 114, 163, 166, 170

Napoleon III, 48
Nemours, 10
Nevers, 2, 5, 14, 17, 21, 117, 128, 129, 130, 131, 138, 139, 140–4, 146, 160
　faïence, 131
　Palais des Ducs, 128
Nod-sur-Seine, 43
Noiset, Claude, 81–2
Nuits-Saint-Georges, 79, 84–5, 138

Paray-le-Monial, 4, 113, 122
Paris, 1, 5, 9, 10, 13, 24, 38, 39, 43, 48, 49, 54, 64, 73, 85, 86, 87, 123, 128, 129, 135, 150, 154, 170, 171
Parker, Kathleen, 66
Perrecy-les-Forges, 124, 125
Petiot, Marcel, 19
phylloxera, 19, 77
Picasso, Pablo, 68
Pierlot, family, 28–9
Pierre-qui-Vire, Abbaye de la, 168–9
Pommard, 79, 93
Poncey, 2
Pontigny, 40
Pont-sur-Yonne, 11, 18
pottery, 26
Pouilly-Fuissé, 2, 118, 136
Pouilly-sur-Loire, 2, 136
Poujade, Robert, 54
Prémery, 135, 145, 146–7
Puligny-Montrachet, 61, 79

Quarré-les-Tombes, 168

Ratilly, 28–30, 51, 134
religion, 7–8
Resistance and Occupation, 1, 7, 26, 85, 96, 122, 126, 128–9, 147, 153, 155, 160
Restif de la Bretonne, 37
Reulle-Vergy, 84
Rochepot, La, 93, 94
Rolin, Jean, 161
Rolin, Nicolas, 89–90, 91, 161
Romans, Gallo-Romans, 6, 11, 13, 16, 18, 21, 25, 31, 32, 37, 48, 55–6, 73, 76, 84, 86, 95, 103, 105, 113, 115, 120, 131, 134, 149, 155, 156, 157, 158, 159, 162, 166, 171

Battle of Alésia, 47–8
roofs, polychrome, 3, 7
Rully, 97

Saint-Amand, 26, 130
Saint-Aubin, 94
Saint-Fargeau, 27–8, 130, 134
Saint-Honoré-les-Bains, 150, 157–8
Saint-Saulge, 145–6, 147
Saint-Sauveur, 30
Saulieu, 166–8
Savigny-lès-Beaune, 85
Schneider, family, 126, 163
Semur-en-Auxois, 42, 44, 49–50
Sens, 2, 10, 12, 13–18, 20, 34
Sercy, 110
Settons, Lac des, 150
Sévigné, Mme de, 131, 164
Sluter, Claus, 57, 65, 66, 73, 74, 146
Solutré, 118–19
Speaight, Robert, 72
stained glass, 15–16, 34, 50, 131, 145
Stendhal, 92, 159–60
Sully, 164–5

Taizé, 111–12
Tanlay, 45, 134
Thénard, Baron, 1
tile-making, 4
Tonnerre, 10, 39, 40–2, 44, 90
Toucy, 31–2
Tournus, 2, 72, 96, 98, 99, 105–9, 113, 117, 118, 123, 131, 161
　Saint-Philibert, 72, 106–7, 109, 113
traboules, 96, 108, 118
Troyes, 17

Valois, dukes of, 6, 7, 57–9, 128
Van der Weyden, Roger, 91
Vauban (Sébastien le Prestre), 170
Vercingetorix, 47, 156
Verdun, 92
Verne, Jules, 84–5
Vézelay, 15, 35, 107, 123, 153, 161, 167, 170, 172, 173, 174–8
Villeneuve-l'Archevêque, 11, 12–13
Villeneuve-sur-Yonne, 18–20, 25

Index

Vix, *vase de*, 44
Volnay, 93
Voltaire, 85
Vosne-Romanée, 1, 79
Vougeot, Clos de, 1, 77, 79, 80, 83

William of Volpiano, 71, 72, 73

wine, 1–2, 21, 23, 32, 33, 38–9, 61, 76–80, 83, 92, 93, 97, 100–1, 131, 136; *see also* village names
wood, 4–5, 18, 26, 123, 151
   market at Château-Chinon, 154
   trade with Lyon, 5, 100
   trade with Paris, 5, 135, 150